Actor Of Life

Actor Of Life

AN UNLIKELY DOCTOR'S
DEFINING MOMENTS

———

Joseph Turcillo Jr., M.D., F.A.C.P.

with Lauren Adamson

ISBN: 1542405807
ISBN 13: 9781542405805
Library of Congress Control Number: 2017900367
CreateSpace Independent Publishing Platform
North Charleston, South Carolina

Dedication

For my cubs, Susie and Lisa, who made my life worth living.

Table of Contents

Part III

Author's Note

THE FOLLOWING MEMOIR DETAILS MEMORABLE and pivotal moments in my personal life and medical career. Many of the names of people from my personal life have been changed to maintain anonymity. All patient names have been changed and some notable or defining characteristics of individual patients have also been modified, in order to preserve patient privacy and doctor-patient confidentiality.

Unfortunately, I did not keep my patients' case notes after retiring and I wrote this memoir many years after my retirement. As such, the facts in the medical cases are described from memory. I made exhaustive efforts to make sure that the essence of each case remains, although some identifying and insignificant details were changed to preserve confidentiality. The conversations shared in this book are accurate to the best of my recollection.

Prologue

Lodi, New Jersey, 1935

I WAS FOUR WHEN MY father was taken away. We were sitting in the cramped living room of our cold water flat when there was a firm knock at the door. Surprised, I looked up at my father, who seemed concerned. It was far past my bedtime, already dark outside; we weren't expecting any visitors. My mother gave him a knowing look and slowly got up and walked to the door, as if she were in trouble. Curious, I ran after her. She opened the door and I was startled to see several policemen. My dad shifted so that he stood in front of me, and I looked up at him in confusion.

"Are you Mr. Turcillo?" one of the policemen barked.

"Yes," my dad said firmly.

"You're under arrest." The officer barged in and began to handcuff my father. The rest was a flurry of overwhelm and screaming. I ran to my dad as he was being taken outside and wrapped myself around his leg, clinging to him, crying for him to stay.

"Don't take away my daddy!" I cried. "Don't take away my daddy!" Tears poured down my face.

I felt hands grabbing me and I clung tighter to my father. One of the policemen slowly removed me from my father's leg and held me back as the two others handcuffed him. I tried to break free by writhing through the officer's grasp, but the large man held me steady with little effort. My father, on the other hand, did not resist at all. My mother rushed over and cradled me as I sobbed. As my father was being escorted out, he turned back to look at us once more with an expression full of regret and sorrow. We watched as they took him out to the police car and drove away. My mom later told me that she saw one of the police officers crying as they separated me from my dad.

My father remained in prison for some time. Why he was there, I really don't know for sure. Apparently, somebody was killed. The authorities thought my father did it. As I got older, I came to understand that the men my dad had worked for were bad people. Who knows what those thugs were thinking. If you did something wrong with them and money was missing, they'd kill you. They had their own honor, their own code.

My mom eventually took me to visit my father in prison. When I first asked him about the arrest, he told me that he never wanted to talk about those things. I respected his wishes and never brought it up. I actually rarely thought about what my father did or wondered if he was guilty. I simply missed him and wished he would come back home.

After he was released from prison, my dad went into hiding and I rarely saw him. For the remainder of his life, he was convinced people were out to get him. Once in a while he'd visit to bring my mother money so we had enough to eat. On these occasions, he would often take me for an ice cream cone. He was proud of me in his own way. It made me happy when he took me different places and said, "This is my son" with a look of pride. He was no angel, but he meant well. One of his favorite things to say – in his thick Jersey accent – was, "There's a lot of good in me, you know?"

Without my father, things were hard on my mother and grandmother. My mom and I eventually moved into another small cold water flat with my grandma. There was no welfare in those days, but somehow my family scraped by. My grandmother did everything she could and worked herself to death. She made heavy coats by hand and sold them to make money to send back to Sicily – everything she did was to help out the family. My mom worked in a factory and also did everything she could to support me, her mom, and my Aunt Lily, who was disabled.

One of my earliest memories is of my mom tucking me in and telling me a bedtime story she made up about two dogs.

In her broken English, my mom began the tale. "There are two dogs, a big dog and a small dog. The big dog was in his doghouse, and the small dog was outside, shivering in the cold."

"Why is he outside?" I asked, concerned.

"Because the big dog won't let him in," she replied.

"Why won't he let him in, Ma?"

"Because the big dog is not being nice to the small dog," she replied flatly.

"Please let the little dog in," I begged.

"Joey, this is just a story," she said with a small laugh and a gentle smile.

"Why can't the little dog come in?" I pleaded, again. I felt a visceral, overwhelming pain thinking of the little dog being kept out.

"He can come in. The big dog changed his mind," my mom said as she began to alter the story. I still remember how upset I felt when I heard that story. Many of my values in life seemed to have been drawn from this story of the "little guy" being bullied. When I got older, I didn't start fights with people, but I would put up a fight for someone who was being taken advantage of.

I don't know how things would have differed if my dad hadn't gone to prison. I suppose things would have been easier. I would have felt safer with his protection, and we would have had more economic stability. My poor mother and grandmother wouldn't have had to work so hard. I know that growing up without my father forced me to become self-reliant, because I wanted to be able to help take care of my family. Yet that self-reliance came with a deep sense of insecurity. It's challenging for a boy to grow up without his father.

As I'd walk around town, sometimes people would ask, "Hey, you Lefty's son?"

"Yes," I'd say, although I never knew why my dad was nicknamed "Lefty." I suppose he was left-handed. His real name was Joseph Turcillo, Sr. Following the typical Italian custom, my parents named me after him.

There were few men I looked up to as a father figure, but I idolized the local doctor, Dr. Catania. Around age seven, I started to realize that Dr. Catania rarely charged us for his visits. I came to understand it was because he was a kind Italian man who knew our situation and knew we couldn't afford the care. I admired his generosity, his professionalism, and was curious about what he did for a living.

I always watched in wonder as Dr. Catania came in our apartment with his black bag. It typically was the same process each time: He would open the bag, get to work, find an ailment, and prescribe a treatment. Then, generally whoever was sick got better. Shortly after these observations and after discovering my love for science, I decided that I wanted to become a doctor like him. I knew that if I became a doctor, I could study a fascinating subject. And more importantly, I could take care of my family and myself.

Part I

———

CHAPTER 1

The Flat

THERE WAS A STRANGE SOUND and a flash that blinded my eyes for a few seconds. I sat there blinking as the photographer adjusted his large camera and the blinding lights. "One more, Joseph," he said with a smile. I looked up again, straight into the camera, with wide eyes and a trembling lip. I felt terrified, though I don't remember why in particular. Probably because the photo was taken right around the time of my dad's arrest. I imagine I was perpetually on edge for a while after that awful night.

My mom framed the portrait and put it out shortly afterward. I've always been sentimental about photographs, even as a child. At some point, I got hold of one of the prints and have always kept a copy of it. Today, I have a print framed in my bedroom. I keep it to remind me of who I was and who, in some ways, I still am. Some early childhood events never truly leave us.

As a child, the predominant feeling I had was loneliness. With my father gone, my mother working long hours at a sweatshop, and no siblings, I longed for more companions. My mom was struggling to keep us afloat without my father in the picture, so we constantly moved around to find cheaper rent. In addition to Lodi, we lived in several flats in the neighboring towns of Garfield and Passaic. It was probably disorienting to move so much as a little kid, but it was simply what I knew and what we had to do, so I didn't think much of it.

*My mom working at a sweatshop – she is just right of center,
in the dark blouse with a stripe around the neckline.*

My schooling was another issue. At the end of third grade, I was pulled into an office where an administrator gently told me that I had to be held back.

"What do you mean?" I asked, confused. The term "held back" was new to me.

"Well, Joseph. You can't read yet. In order to pass the third grade, you need to meet certain requirements, one of which is basic reading..." she trailed off. I fell silent. My mom couldn't read; there wasn't anyone at home to help me learn.

When I got home, I cried to my mother as I explained my situation. I cried so much that the following day, she held my hand as we marched into the principal's office. She adamantly protested their decision to hold me back. I remember sitting there, my cheeks reddening as my mom spoke in broken English, making her case for me to proceed to the fourth grade. To this day, I'm not sure how much the principal understood.

I appreciated her fierce efforts to defend me, but she was unable to sway the administration. The following year, I treaded back into third grade, feeling ashamed, but more determined to learn. I put my head in the books and kept trying. Fortunately, public schools were good in those days, and I had effective teachers. Once I did learn to read, it was a wonder. The loneliness I had typically felt as a small child began to lift as I started filling some of my spare time with learning. I didn't have much growing up, but I did have ambition. Besides, I lacked a radio and television, or any other electronic distractions. Studying science was truly one of the most exciting ways to pass my alone time.

Despite the early struggles, we caught a break when we landed in a place I learned to call home: 45 Harrison Avenue in Garfield, New Jersey. It was a cold water flat in the Italian part of town. What I loved about it was that we lived with some of my extended family: Dona Grazia (my grandmother), Aunt Lily, Aunt Josie and Uncle Joe, and my cousins Johnny and Annie.

My mom, grandma, and Aunt Lily lived in the front of the flat, and Annie's family lived in the back. Annie was closer to me in age, about two and a half years older. Johnny was four years older than I and loved to do anything that involved physical activity. Since I didn't have any brothers and sisters, I loved having Annie and Johnny around to play with. The sense of community was the brightest aspect of my childhood.

One of the best parts about living at 45 Harrison was having our grandmother around. She had the biggest heart and was the most hardworking woman I ever met. I often think about how I wish she hadn't needed to work so hard. All of her time was either spent making coats (so that she could send money back home to our family in Sicily) or cooking from scratch. My grandma made the most incredible Italian meals and pastries. She even made her own wine in our basement.

As a kid, my favorite things were the Christmas cakes she used to make. When I came home, all bundled up from being outside in the December chill, I could smell the sweet, buttery scent of the cakes as soon as I opened our front door. They were made with figs and raisins, and she made a huge number of them to give out to the neighbors who would congregate at our home for prayer meetings or simply to socialize.

At one point, my cousins and I discovered that she let them cool on her bed, over a white bedspread, most likely so that we wouldn't pick at them.

Once we found out where they were kept, we all snuck up to eat some of the cakes, as children are wont to do.

Given that my grandma did so much around the house, there was little for me to do in terms of housework. However, I did heat up water for our baths. In a cold water flat, we had to put a pot of water on a coal fire stove, heat the pot, bring it to the bathtub (since the running water was all cold), and mix it up with cold water. Then I'd soap myself up and dump the water over my head with a bucket.

Apart from that, I didn't do many chores. Whenever something needed to be fixed, especially if it was dangerous in any way, my mother would always say, "Let Johnny do it." I never thought much about it at the time; it just made sense, given that Johnny was quite a bit older and liked helping out.

Sometimes, in families, it seems that we unconsciously fill roles that we see missing. My mom and grandma brought in the money (though we were always struggling to have enough of it) and had the meals and cleaning taken care of. Johnny would fix things. Annie would help out around the house as well. I was the baby of the extended family, so I was cut more slack. But I used much of that free time to learn. I realized that if I became a doctor, I could help my family by taking care of their medical needs and providing for them financially.

Since I spent a lot of time alone, I got used to learning how to do various things on my own. As a little kid, I would go to the YMCA in Passaic, which was right across the street from the apartment we were living in at the time. At around ten years old, I saw others swimming and wanted to join, so I figured I would teach myself how to swim. That worked out fine in the shallow end, but once I ventured into the deep end, I realized I was literally in over my head—I started to sink. Thankfully, someone noticed I was drowning and jumped in to save me.

The next time I went to the pool, I went back in the shallow end. I wasn't going to go in deep water until I learned how to swim. It didn't occur to me to ask someone else to teach me how to do it, so I just got in the shallow end and practiced. I propelled myself with my feet pushing off the bottom and my head and arms in the water, basically half walking and half swimming with my arms.

Soon enough I got better at floating and swimming along with my legs kicking behind me. I pretended I was in the deep end, and once my confidence was up, I gradually progressed to deeper water. Eventually, I was delighted to find myself swimming in the deep end. That's how I solved all my problems in life: I tried different ways of tackling a challenge, and when something worked, I continued with it. I kept tinkering until I got it right.

As time went by, I became proficient at different strokes and wanted a new challenge. I started eyeing the diving boards with a mix of enthusiasm and hesitation. I noticed some older kids diving off the high boards, which looked fun and impressive. More importantly, the girls admired the guys who went off the high board. The only problem was that I was afraid of heights. Even the little lynchpin board seemed daunting.

Each time I walked along that little board and thought about going in headfirst, I abandoned that plan, jumping off of it, too afraid to dive in. After a few times of intending to dive, but jumping instead, I told myself I had to dive. The swimming was just the beginning; I was determined to dive off that board. I had to do it because all the girls would be looking at me.

Knowing the girls were watching was enough motivation, and off I went, headfirst into the water. It took some time before my form was decent, but once it was, I decided to learn some new tricks. On the small boards I learned how to do a jackknife dive and wasn't afraid doing it.

The more I dove, the more I figured I could do. I kept eying the ten-foot board, determined to dive off of it. Jumping off the ten-foot board was no problem. It was going headfirst that was an issue. Just like with the smaller board, I had a mental block that held me back.

Everybody has his own fear. Fear is largely an illusion – most of the things we fear in life don't ever happen – but I didn't know that then. However, I asked myself: If I can jump forward, why can't I jump backward? Then I started jumping backward and I noticed that sometimes I was almost doing a back dive, because I wasn't landing straight. I suppose that because gravity was bringing me closer to diving as I jumped, I mustered up the courage to go with that force and go headfirst.

Eventually I was able to do a jackknife on the ten-foot board. So I progressed into a back jackknife. Once I did that, it was like virtual reality – and I could do it without fear. Next I did a front jackknife. After that came a double jackknife. After that, a jackknife into a swan. There was nothing holding me back!

Next I went to the fifteen-foot board and then a higher board, the twenty-foot board. And nothing could stop me because I knew I had nothing to fear; it's water down there! And that's how I did everything in life – step by step, my way. Taking a page from my idol, Frank Sinatra, I did it my way – the only way I could do it. Sometimes the best way to learn something is to teach ourselves, to learn by trial and error.

Nevertheless, I was always happy to have certain people teach me. Anytime my cousin Johnny wanted to teach me something, I was excited to learn from him. After all, he was the family member I most looked up to as a boy. Since I barely saw my father, Johnny was the one I tended to go to for advice. Way before it was popular, Johnny was a sort of health nut. He always told me the importance of exercise and nutrition.

"Don't smoke and don't drink, Joey," Johnny would lecture me. He knew smoking was bad for you long before it was a truism. When he told me not to smoke, I listened – at least for a while, because he was like my protector. Johnny was tall and incredibly fit – quite a specimen. He should have been a movie actor. But he went into fighting instead – he began boxing and later became a prizefighter, even winning the Diamond Glove. But long before he won anything, I saw him as a big brother and some sort of hero. He taught me how to exercise and took me boxing a few times. I didn't particularly take to it but enjoyed him training me. The best part was just hanging around with him; I felt happy and safe when I was with him.

Johnny called the polluted river near where we lived "Zoda's Pond." And he'd get pissed off at anybody who threw things in the river and further contaminated the water. We used to swim at Saddle River, in an area we called "The Pum House." Johnny was always pushing the limits and would climb a tree that branched out over the swimming hole, then dive straight into the shallow water.

Being the character that he was, Johnny once decided to sport a loincloth and played Tarzan in the trees. He'd smack his chest and holler until I cracked up in laughter. Then he'd dive into the water. I always held my breath until he surfaced again, worried he'd hit the bottom. Fortunately, he never did.

Cousin Johnny

One day we were all at a neighborhood pool, and a few older guys started picking on me. Johnny defended me, and one of the other guys took a swing at Johnny, who caught the punch with his hand and gave the guy a look of pity before throwing a punch himself. His opponent probably didn't know Johnny was a boxer and only put up a brief fight before Johnny knocked him out. The other guys who had chastised me looked at their unconscious friend, then back up at Johnny, who flashed a menacing grin and yelled, "Who's next?" They all turned on their heels and ran the other way.

Johnny wasn't very interested in school. Fortunately, I was, but partially because I felt I didn't have much else to do. As a little kid, I remember playing with toys and reading a lot, especially in the winter, when I was snowed in. The littlest things would excite me in those days – such as a science book or a new type of food to try. We typically ate a "poor man's diet" of eggs, beans, potatoes, and Italian food. On the rare occasion that I had some extra cash, I'd treat my friends to a pizza at Barcelona's Bar and Grill, which was a restaurant right across the street from our flat. When I was a kid, it cost one dollar for an entire pizza at Barcelona's.

But we mostly stuck to homemade food. I remember when I tried chocolate pudding for the first time. Uncharacteristically, my mom had made something new. It was a hot day and the cool, creamy chocolate pudding was the perfect dessert to have. After tasting it, I couldn't contain my excitement and threw open the window, yelling, "Look at me! I have chocolate pudding" to the people passing by.

Another time my mom brought home some Silvercup bread. I'd never seen sliced bread before and found it odd that it was pre-cut, unlike the loaves of bread my grandma made from scratch. My mom gave me a slice, and I was fascinated by how light and fluffy it was. When you can be thrilled by a piece of sliced bread, it doesn't take much to find some joy. Growing up with so little was a hardship, but it made the small pleasures in life stand out in a striking manner.

CHAPTER 2

Street Kids

———

OUTSIDE OF THE FLAT AND school, I spent most of my time on the streets. Growing up, my best friends were Lou Russo, Horace DeTecco and Joe Bosco. Lou was as smart as a whip, always acing his math tests. His father ran his own small business as a baker and they lived just above their shop, right down the street from me. Horace was the kindest guy you'd want to meet – always doing favors for others. Joe Bosco, on the other hand, was a rascal – the purest rascal on earth. If people ever started talking about values, he'd grimace and say, "Don't get dramatic." We lived on a good Italian street, complete with a group of street kids who we simply called "the gang."

Although we didn't get into too much trouble, we were what you would call a Jersey street gang. At times, we fought with other street gangs, getting into minor brawls or hurling rocks at each other. I don't remember anyone getting hurt all that badly, though of course there were some fistfights and all of that. Some of the guys in our gang were really tough. If you were walking down the street and looked at them the wrong way, they'd beat you up. We had a tendency to congregate on certain street corners, sitting on a stoop smoking and shooting the shit with each other. Basically, we were just passing the time. I was never one to initiate a fight, but I would defend myself or fight if I had to.

Some of the older guys in my street gang

One time, some members of a nearby gang started beating me up, completely out of the blue. I tried to fight back, but knew it was no use, as I was being taken on by about five other guys. They didn't cause too much damage, though I had some black and blue bruises and hurt quite a bit for a week or so. I didn't ask why they did it; I suppose I just knew it wasn't really anything personal; it was simply a way for them to get out some pent up aggression and boredom.

Most of the time, though, we were just roughhousing or having a good time together. There was a game we used to play called Shiney, which involved hitting things around with a broomstick. Our favorite sport was touch football, which was actually my greatest joy growing up. We used to play on the grass fields by Holy Name Church and I would completely lose track of time as we ran around tossing the football. There was something so freeing about the sport.

The stresses of daily life typically felt bearable as long as I had my football games. The only time I got hurt badly was when a buddy of mine and I were running toward the same pass and ended up smacking our heads into each other. I got knocked out and had to be stitched up. All the guys came to the house to visit me afterward. Those are the kind of people they were. I mean they were rough but they had a sense of honor. I was just a kid; they took care of the kid.

The injury didn't keep me away from football for long. It was probably only a few days until I was out on the field again, running around with my buddies. I used to get so mad at my mother, coming after me at the fields, yelling, "Joey, come home and eat!" I wondered why she wouldn't leave me alone and let me play. Sometimes I was really mad when she insisted I return home. I was playing with the guys and didn't want her nagging me.

Although my mom and I were very close, there were times she would lose her temper with me. As hard as my mom worked, trudging through the snow even when she was sick, just to put food on the table, I didn't understand the sacrifices she was making. At times, raising me alone got to be too much and she'd send me off to spend a few days with other relatives. When times were particularly hard, she had me actually live with other relatives for short periods.

While I didn't like having to live away from my mom, I loved seeing different aunts and uncles, particularly because they had bigger families and I loved spending time with my cousins. My favorite aunt was my Aunt Marie. I always went to her house around Christmastime for a few days. She lived a bus ride away, in Saddle River, and had three boisterous boys: Carmin, Gerard, and Sam. Carmin rode motorcycles and would take me out for rides at times, which made me think of him as my cool older cousin. They were all quite a bit older than me and I looked up to each one of them.

When I was a little kid, the three brothers had a routine every time I was returning to my mom's. They would ask me if I stole anything. Their family had a lot more than my mom did, so they thought I might be tempted to steal. Their question was partially a joke, but like many jokes, there was some real concern behind it.

I'd always tell them, "No, you're my family. I'd never steal from you."

Then one of them would say something like, "Well, let's make sure" and they'd all get a mischievous look on their faces. Then they'd grab me, turn me upside down, and shake me to ensure there wasn't anything in my pockets. We'd all laugh until they were satisfied I was clean, at which point they would turn me right side up and let me go.

Later on, the three brothers were sent to New Guinea to fight in World War II. I'd go over to the house every Saturday and listen to the radio with my Aunt Marie and my cousin Gerard's wife, Jay. Those days huddled by the radio helped us form a sort of camaraderie, rooting for our boys. We listened to Lucky Strike Radio and heard Frank Sinatra singing, which kept us all together. I thought of my cousins in New Guinea and wondered what it was like to be at war. I was warm, in Aunt Marie's house, often enjoying a Sunday dinner with her and Jay, but I had no idea what it was like for my cousins halfway across the world.

The closest thing I'd ever experience was when I started a Marine Cadet club with my buddies and we'd hold meetings in Lou's basement. We'd pretend to be Marines, tumbling over each other and taking turns playing the commander who pointed to various parts of the map and invented battle instructions. But we all seriously wanted to be Marines for quite some time. My father, who'd been in the Navy, once bought me a Marine Cadet uniform and I wore it at our club meetings. But long before I turned eighteen, I lost interest in joining the Marines and had my sights set on college.

Sometimes, when I was sent to live with different aunts and uncles in my youth, it was an unpleasant experience. As a kid, I always missed my mom when we were apart for more than a few days. The most difficult separation was when she sent me to Pennsylvania to live with some cousins on a farm. I think I was around five at the time. My mom chose to send me off to the farm after she once hyperbolically said something like, "I'm going to die," probably in reference to how overrun she felt and I replied, "Go ahead and die." I didn't know what I was saying; I loved her dearly, but I was a street kid. She hoped that living on the farm for a while and doing hard labor away from the streets would help straighten me out. I suppose it did, to some degree. At the very least, I was more careful about the way I spoke to her once I returned home.

My mom hardly ever hit me, but I do recall a couple of times where she really gave it to me. In one incident, some company came over and I was playing with a new toy I had just bought with my own money. All of a sudden, my mom took the toy and handed it to the couple's child to play with. I didn't want anyone to take my toy – I had saved for a while to buy it. I started crying, thinking my mom was giving it away.

"I worked for the money to buy that! Don't give it to anyone else," I cried. My mom got very upset with me and told me to share. She took me aside and whacked the hell out of me while telling me not to be selfish.

Another time she cornered me in a hallway, but I don't remember what this beating was for. But all of a sudden she was smacking me: boom, boom, boom, left and right. I wasn't scared, but I desperately wanted to get away from her blows. I think I intuitively understood my poor mom was hurting herself, just striking back at life. And I guess I represented life, in a way. It's terrible that a mother would have to suffer and even take things out on her child. But my mother's life was hard and the kind of upbringing she had came with regular beatings.

And as loving as she was, I think she got that anger from her father. She told me the story about how, back in Sicily, her father once asked her to get him something but she was busy and noticed her sister, Josie, sitting around leisurely. So she suggested, "Why don't you ask Josie to do it? She's not doing anything." But boy, was that a mistake. My grandfather stood up, towering above my tiny mother, and glared at her before smacking her on one side of the face with the palm of his hand, then the other side with the back of his hand.

He waited a moment to let the blows sink in, then simply said, "I asked you to do it" and sat back down. So I'm guessing that's where she got it. How you treat your children will affect how they treat other people. I never forget that.

My mom was born in Boston but after only a year or so, was taken back to Sicily, where she lived on a rural farm with her family. Growing up there, she didn't learn English, which was why she never properly learned to read and write in English (or even speak it fluently). It must have been an interesting time, growing up in Sicily, especially with the type of family she had. Her father was a real son of a gun, from what I hear. He was accused of killing a man. Somebody tried to hustle one of his daughters, supposedly. From the way he was described, it appeared he didn't know any fear.

My mother was brave, raising me alone. She rarely spoke about what a struggle it was, but one time, we were walking to a friend's apartment and before we rang the doorbell, she sat down and started crying.

"What's wrong, Ma?" I asked, confused about her sadness.

She looked up at me and slowly replied, "I'm tired, Joey. Tired of working so hard." Although I was just a kid, it struck me that my mom was exhausted and I empathized with her. My poor mother, who did she have to depend on? Who did she have to fall back on? I was just a kid. She couldn't rely on me. What did I know? When I think of my mom and what she went through, I think of how so many mothers go through hell for their babies. Even in the animal kingdom. As I grew older, I learned to appreciate my mom and felt incredibly indebted to her. I knew that I needed to get a job that would allow me to take care of her, which was a large part of the reason I wanted to be a doctor. That way I could provide for her, make her proud, and monitor her health, just as she had always done her best to take care of me.

CHAPTER 3

The Palace

———

For as long as I can remember, films have entranced me. I was about eight when my mom gave me a movie ticket to the Ritz Theater so I could go see a film on a Saturday afternoon. The ticket cost ten cents back then. We rarely went to the movies and I was thrilled to have something different to do that day. I was happily walking toward downtown Garfield when I saw a group of older kids in their mid teens walking toward me. They were of the street gang variety, though they seemed rougher than my friends.

One of them eyed me and elbowed his buddy as he said something I couldn't make out. I felt a lurch in my stomach. I glanced over my shoulder, hoping they were looking at someone else behind me, but I was the only one on the block. Keeping my eyes down, I tried to walk past them when one of them stepped in front of me so that I walked right into his torso.

"Hey! Watch it!" he yelled with a smirk. His friends began to snicker.

"Sorry," I replied, trying to side step around him, when he grabbed both of my shoulders and said, "Where d'ya think you're going, kid?"

"The theater," I said meekly.

"The theater?" he replied mockingly. "Do you have a ticket?"

"Yes."

"Lemme see it, then." I didn't know what else to do, so I slowly took my ticket out of my pocket. He snatched it from me and eyed it over.

"Hey, Larry, look at this," he said as he nudged his friend. "This ticket's no good!"

"Ah, yer right. That ticket's no good," his friend confirmed, shaking his head.

"Well, give it back to me then," I said.

"It's no good, no sense in having it," the boy who stopped me said. But something in me told me the ticket was mine to keep.

"My mom gave it to me. I know it's good. Give it back," I said sternly. The older boys started to laugh at me.

"Suit yourself, kid," he said as he took the ticket and held it out in front of me. I hesitated a moment, thinking he would pull it back just as I was about to grab it, but I slowly reached out and he let me take the ticket. Once I had it, I started running off toward the theater. The guys laughed at me, but I kept sprinting without looking back.

Once I made it to the theater, I was panting as I gave my ticket to the usher waiting at the door.

"Afternoon, son," he said, chipper.

"Good afternoon, Sir," I replied, holding my breath as I waited to see if he'd accept the ticket. In truth, I wasn't completely sure if it was a good ticket. But my spirits lifted as I watched the usher tear off part of the ticket and hand the stub back to me.

"Enjoy the show," he said with a smile. I grinned and took the ticket, holding my head a bit higher as I walked into the theater.

Growing up, movies were a beautiful escape from reality and gave me a sense of how grand life could potentially become. Movies were different back then; they had a sense of right and wrong and good usually prevailed. During the Depression, people needed an escape from the harsh realities of daily living and the movies were the place most people went to hide out from the world for a few hours.

I believe all the romance films I saw also turned me into the romantic I became at a young age. Even as an eight year old, while many of my friends still thought girls were gross, I started daydreaming about having a girlfriend. And about sex, though I didn't know how it worked at the time. The first girl I had a crush on was named Bridgette and she was a neighbor of ours. I got the idea that I should give her a present, so I put together some candy and walked over to her door. As an eight year old, I didn't know what I was doing in the least bit, but I just wanted to be near her, and candy seemed like the best thing to give a young girl. I pressed the doorbell and stood there with the box of candy in my hand, my heart pounding.

As soon as I heard footsteps coming toward the door, I panicked. It sounded like a man's heavy stomps and I wondered who her father was and what he would say when he saw me standing on the porch. Without giving it any thought, I practically dropped the candy and ran as fast as I could around the corner. I heard the door open and a man say, "Hello?" as I squatted around the side of the house, holding my breath so I wouldn't make a sound. Once I heard the door close, I sprinted home.

I was panting as I rushed into the flat and saw our family friend (who would later become my godfather) was there for a surprise visit. In our culture, people didn't have to call ahead to drop by, they would just stop in and they were welcome for a cup of coffee and a snack. He asked me what I was up to and chuckled at my flushed cheeks and palpable anxiety. After I explained my attempt to give Bridgette the candy, he laughed mercilessly. I stared silently, waiting for him to explain what was so funny about my predicament. He must have said something like, "Joey! You're not supposed to drop it and run! You gotta hand the candy to her and start a conversation."

My romantic tendencies were probably really ingrained later on, though, when I became a movie usher, at around age fourteen, at a local theater. The place was inaptly named The Palace, given that it was a complete hole in the wall. The Palace was on Market Street in Passaic, which was about twenty miles away from our flat in Garfield. I would ride my bike that distance each way. Back then, bikes didn't have the kinds of gears they have today, so it was a great workout that made my leg muscles powerful. In the winter, biking was no longer an option, so I would take a few buses to the theater.

Although the commute could be grueling, I loved the job, mainly because I got to see every movie for free. When I watched those movies, I was completely entranced. I lived through them all. I was always falling in love, like the protagonists I saw on the big screen. After a few years of working as an usher, I was promoted to Head Usher, which made me hold my head a bit higher.

This promotion made me proud enough to walk up to a girl I liked and say, "I don't want to brag, but, I'm Head Usher at the movie theater." Though I don't remember her reaction – I only remember my statement because it's laughable – I can't imagine she was that impressed.

As I sat in the movie house, I often dreamt of being a movie star and seeing my picture on the screen like my heroes. I was an usher for about four or five years. All the movies I saw also helped me become a more social being, in a way, because I was always copying the heroes in the movies – trying to mimic their mannerisms and charisma.

Growing up, I had three dream careers. One was to become a doctor, the other was to become a movie actor, and the third was to become a pilot. Since I had (and still have) a terrible fear of flying, I guess being an actor would have been the next best option. Although I loved the idea of acting and did participate in some high school plays, I felt my voice, diction, and grammar were too poor for me to be a movie actor.

Truly, I didn't have the prerequisites to become any of these things. In some ways, attempting to become a doctor was the loftiest option of them all, given how challenging it is academically. But I loved science and the idea of being able to intelligently manage my health and take care of my family led me to pursue that path.

Nevertheless, I still always had show business and a dream of acting in the back of my mind. That's what later led me to practice medicine in Los Angeles and pursue relationships with singers and actresses. Besides, my biggest heroes weren't doctors. I mostly looked up to Frank Sinatra and the big actors of the day, like Cary Grant.

In some sense, I think all the movies I watched gave me a warped perspective on life and unreasonable expectations for reality, particularly in the area of love. I've always wanted those cinematic romances, those perfect women that make sense on a two-dimensional screen but don't represent the complexity of women in our real, three-dimensional world.

But I watched so many goddamn movies that I believed in them and was always looking for that romance that would captivate me so completely that it would save me from fear and eliminate any insecurities – the kind of love where you can only be in the present moment, which is always euphoric, and therefore immune to the many unpleasant parts of reality.

CHAPTER 4

An Education

———

LOU WAS A GOOD INFLUENCE on me because he was very devoted to and enthusiastic about his math and science studies. I didn't know anybody else my age as diligent as him. Although I loved science and enjoyed school, I was actually failing out of Passaic High School when I was halfway through tenth grade, so I ended up switching to Garfield High and started tenth grade over with a clean slate.

When I got there, I was in school with Lou and I think that helped put me on a better path. Lou was a year ahead and in that sense, I looked up to him. At Garfield High I fell in love with science even more when I took chemistry. The course fascinated me and I became quite adept at it. Still, my focus at this age was far more on my friends and girls than in the classroom.

I turned a new leaf when I started at Garfield High. For whatever reason, I wanted to be as involved as possible, so I signed up for as many clubs and events as I could. I joined the track team, yearbook, and theater club. Growing up I was yearning to be noticed so I engaged in everything high school had to offer, trying to get in every picture for the yearbook.

Horace, my first childhood friend, lived nearby too but was less interested in school than Lou and me. His attention primarily went into his work – he was a complete maniac for cars. Horace would examine any car he could get his hands on and started working at car shops, fixing up different vehicles. When he got a bit older, he ended up buying cars dirt cheap, fixing them up himself, then selling them for a profit. I always admired Horace's cars and longed to have my own.

Around age sixteen, I remember waiting for the bus outside of the neighborhood public pool when a beautiful red convertible pulled up in front of me. But I only admired the car for a split second before realizing there was a gorgeous girl behind the wheel. She was stopped at the red light but looked my way and offered a small smile before looking back at the road. She seemed to be around my age, but I had never seen her before. Without thinking about it, I got up from the bench and swiftly walked over to her.

"Excuse me, I gotta ask you something," I said with a grin, slipping my hands into my pockets.

She beamed back at me and said, "What's that?" I paused briefly, knowing I had to say something. I couldn't just let this stunning girl drive away without giving it a shot.

"How does a guy like me meet a girl like you?" I asked in complete sincerity. The second I said it I wondered if it had been a complete blunder, a ridiculous thing to ask a perfect stranger.

"Have your mother call my mother for an introduction," she replied without missing a beat, as if that were the standard practice. I stood there, dumbfounded, as she pulled a little notepad and pen out of her dash, jotting her number down. After delicately ripping it off the notepad, she handed it to me, smiled, then drove off.

I stood there with the paper in my hand, knowing that I would never ask my mother to call. We were from different worlds. My mom spoke in broken English and was illiterate. Her mother was probably refined and well educated. She was zipping around town in a nice convertible, while I was waiting on the side of the road to take two busses back home to a run down flat.

On the bus rides back, I daydreamed about that girl, whose name I never knew. She reminded me of the beautiful actresses I saw in the movies. I fantasized about where she might live, what it would be like to have a girlfriend like that, and what it would be like to own a car like hers. At that time, I didn't have a girlfriend or a car of any kind.

When I was seventeen, I ended up buying my first car from Horace. It was a Chevy (we called it a General) and I bought it for $20. I actually didn't even pay Horace for it; we simply agreed that I would pay him $20 when I could.

It was a complete piece of crap – I had to hit the ignition with a hammer to get the thing to start – but it was mine and I was delighted to have a car. And although it was run down and the paint was quite worn, it was technically a red convertible. But that didn't keep me from being self conscious about rolling around town in such a piece of junk. I felt that people might be laughing at me. I figured I'd add to their amusement and literally painted on a sign that read: "Don't laugh at this car...your daughter may be in it."

My first car, parked outside of 45 Harrison Ave

And I did take out quite a few girls in that car. I was incredibly girl crazy from a young age. When it came to wooing girls, I looked up to some older guys in the gang and my buddy Joe Bosco. Sometimes I went on double dates with Joe and he had the most gorgeous girls, the ones you thought were untouchable – but he would touch them. Joe Bosco didn't care what people thought; he ended up going on our weeklong senior trip (to Washington D.C.) with nothing but a toothbrush.

My buddies and I were lectured on how to romance a girl from the older kids in our street gang, particularly one older guy named Redovella, or "Red" for short. That guy had a way with the ladies, though in retrospect, it's hard to understand how girls fell for his antics. I'll never forget about one piece of advice Red gave us in particular. I must have been about fifteen when he told a group of us, in his thick Jersey accent, "Now, guys, you gotta know what to say to a chick." He took a deep drag of his cigarette. We hung on his every word – after all, he was one of the cool older guys who would strut around town with a beautiful girl on his arm.

"This is what you gotta say. You gotta look in the girl's eyes, wait a minute," he paused dramatically and took another drag as we waited on the edge of our seats for his advice. He smiled slyly and finally revealed his secret: "Then tell her, 'Baby, don't cha know? Don't cha believe I love ya?'"

Thankfully, I never actually tried that line on a girl. Despite my naiveté, I had enough sense to realize what a ridiculous thing that was to say to a girl I had just met. Nevertheless, it seemed to work for Red. We were young kids, mostly raising ourselves on the streets, who didn't receive much advice about how to pursue and treat women. I never saw any of these guys hurt a girl physically, but like most guys our age, we had one thing on our mind and would say pretty much anything to get in a girl's pants.

For me, it was different. Not that I didn't want to get in their pants – I wanted that very much – but it was also about romance. All those years of sitting in the cinema, watching the grand romances made a huge impression on me. I think I was also hungry for more attention and love. As a small child, I spent so much of the day alone, because I didn't have siblings. Although my mom did as much as she could for me, she worked most of the time, which often left me feeling lonely. I craved a woman's affection, but not only in a physical sense. I wanted a connection and a consistent companion.

When I asked girls out, I typically asked them out to the ice cream parlor. We'd have an ice cream cone, then I'd suggest we dance. After putting a coin in the jukebox and selecting one of my favorite songs, I'd hold out my hand to the girl and lead her to slow dance near the jukebox.

I also enjoyed singing to girls. When we would walk far for a date, I'd end up singing to them most of the way home. In retrospect, I don't know if they necessarily liked that or not, but at least some of them seemed to enjoy my enthusiasm.

From a young age, I always seemed to be falling in love. By that, I mean infatuation and puppy love, although as I grew a little older, I had my first serious girlfriend. Her name was Jean Daul. Jean was a classy girl who lived in Wallington, which was the town next to Garfield that was mostly Polish at the time. I think I met her at the Polish People's House, which was a social club that hosted dances that I frequented.

We may have been together a year, which was the longest I had dated a girl at that time. When she dumped me, I was heartbroken, but I didn't blame her. I was a young kid and felt I didn't have much to offer. Although I pined after her for a while, I ended up seeing other girls and losing track of Jean. In hindsight, I think about all the women I dated who I lost track of and feel it's a shame that there are some people we grow so close to, then completely lose touch with.

Despite the fact that I dated many women and wasn't afraid to put myself out there, I was still deeply shy in certain ways. And I often felt I couldn't have the girls I most wanted. I remember lusting after the high school cheerleaders, who I never even spoke to because they all dated the football players. What would they want to do with me? I asked myself and resigned to the belief that they wouldn't give me the time of day. So I moved on to the women I thought I had a chance with.

There was a time, when I was eighteen, that I was interested in this woman named Lucy and it became clear that we could be a sure thing. Lucy was a sophisticated, sexy chick and all the guys in our gang were interested in her. For whatever reason, she was interested in me, which caught me by surprise – and elicited sheer delight.

Lucy wore dresses and heels, red lipstick, and smoked cigarettes. I didn't smoke because my cousin Johnny had told me not to, and it didn't particularly appeal to me. Seeing this beautiful woman with her cigarettes did appeal to me, though, and it automatically made me think of all the Hollywood bomb-shells who smoked heavily in films.

The day I knew I would see Lucy and felt we were a sure thing, I knew I needed to be prepared. Lou walked with me to the drug store but when I went in, there was – to my horror – a woman at the cash register.

"Lou!" I whispered, "I can't buy them! It's a *woman*." The idea of buying prophylactics was embarrassing enough if I had to buy them from a man, but to buy them from a young woman was unbearable.

"So what?" he said with a laugh. Lou was anything but shy. "People buy them all the time."

"I can't do it. Will you do it for me?" I pleaded, holding out some cash.

"You really won't do it?" he replied with a chuckle, seeming to think I was acting childishly. But I wouldn't, and after some persuading, Lou shrugged and made the purchase without any fear or shame. I had to admire his confidence as he handed me the bag and rolled his eyes a little with a smile.

That night we went out with Lucy and some of her friends. At some point, Lucy and I split off and went for a walk in the park while our friends waited a few blocks down in the car. We walked over to a tree and Lucy stood against it and took out a pack of cigarettes. She daintily poured one out, offered it to me, and I politely declined. As she lit her cigarette under the starlight it illuminated her face and I tried not to let my nerves show.

She started smoking and the scent of it hit me instantly. When she was done with the cigarette, we spoke a bit, then started kissing. I tasted the cigarette on her lips and the memory was seared into my brain. I'll always have a fond memory of kissing her against the tree and of how things progressed. Finally I pulled out the prophylactic I had been afraid to buy and made love to Lucy against the tree. Afterwards, I put the prophylactic back in its wrapper and ended up putting it in a scrapbook.

Although I didn't date Lucy very long, I'll always remember her, especially because of the way she smoked. After being with her, I've always had a Pavlovian response when I'm in close proximity with an attractive chick puffing a cigarette. From a health perspective, I don't like smoking. Yet when I'm beside a beautiful woman and take in the scent of her cigarette, my mind invariably wanders back to that night with Lucy.

CHAPTER 5

An Honest Day's Work

———

I HAD A NUMBER OF odd jobs growing up, and though I hated some of them at the time, I'd do them all over again in a heartbeat. Even in the most mundane positions, I learned something valuable. My very first job was shining shoes. I was nine years old and I believe I got that job through a friend, possibly Horace, whose father repaired shoes. The job didn't last long, however, because not many people in my neighborhood needed their shoes shined. Or there wasn't enough extra cash to justify that small luxury.

Shortly after the announcement of Pearl Harbor, I began bagging groceries, when I was ten. While that job wasn't particularly memorable, it's interesting to think about how no nine or ten year old could legally work a job like that today (at least not in the U.S.).

The most tiring job of my youth was working the milk route. I was twelve or thirteen when I began and the job was grueling – I had to get up at three o'clock in the morning to start delivering the milk. My friend Horace did this with me. Back then, milk was delivered in the early morning hours to peoples' doorsteps. The milkman, Phil, would drive his truck very slowly and Horace and I would take the crate of milk and run it to a doorstep, then pick up the crate of empty bottles and run it back to the truck to get another full crate and repeat the process going down the street. This was easiest when delivering to people on the ground floor in good weather. In the winter, I trudged through the snow and up long, cold flights of stairs carting peoples' milk while they were sound asleep.

Sometimes I'd be out late with my buddies and would barely sleep an hour or two before starting the route. When one of our older buddies drove us back from a night out, I could unequivocally be found sleeping in the back seat because the early morning hours just killed me. I told myself one day, I'll be able to sleep in.

There were a few times, after late nights, that I delivered milk to the wrong places and upset my boss. For the most part, I delivered everything correctly, though a bit begrudgingly. To make the job a little more pleasant, I started drinking some cream while I was working. It tasted great and it was free, so I figured why not drink it? After a while, I started developing chest pains and wondered if it was the cream. To test it out, I told myself I'd stop drinking it for a few days and see if I noticed any changes in my chest. Sure enough, when I stopped drinking the cream, the chest pain decreased as well, and then I was back at square one with a healthy heart but no perks to the job.

Being an usher was one of my favorite jobs growing up. I did well in jobs that didn't require too much physical labor, such as being an usher or working in a hospital. The worst I ever did on a job was when I worked as a carpenter for a few weeks. I shortly got sick as hell and was unable to work for weeks. I quickly realized that I wasn't built for those kinds of jobs; I simply didn't have the endurance for them. Even in high school, I was on the track team, but not as a distance runner – I did field events like pole vault and high jump. And I wasn't good at that either. But I did enjoy it and I got my picture in the yearbook.

Part of the reason for my lack of endurance was probably because I did so much between school, extracurricular activities, work, seeing my gang, and chasing girls. For a long period in high school, I spent every Friday night going out dancing with my buddies. We'd cruise to the outskirts of town, about fifteen miles from Garfield, to our favorite spot: Nolan's. Although it was a simple bar way out in the wilderness, it was the most happening place nearby, so we nicknamed it Club Nolan. There were a few reasons Nolan's became our go to place: they had a great jukebox and dance floor. Another reason we returned to Club Nolan so religiously was that it had a large parking lot, where we could spend time with girls in our cars.

Our routine was simple: gather the gang, cruise up to Club Nolan's, park and wait for the girls, make out with the girls in the car, then go in and dance.

Nolan's was a pretty nondescript place, not quite a dive but also nothing that nice. It was perfect for a bunch of high school kids looking to have a fun time away from home.

Dancing has been one of my favorite pastimes ever since I started teaching myself in middle school. Initially I didn't know what I was doing, but I always loved it – the movement, the music, the laughter. In the early days, I would carefully observe the older guys who could dance well and remember their moves, then try them out myself. I kept repeating that process until girls would compliment me, then I got courageous enough to try some of my own moves and to stop watching others for guidance. Eventually I became so confident in my dancing that nothing held me back. If I asked a girl to dance and she was reluctant, or said she wasn't very good, I'd extend my hand and tell her, "Don't worry. I can make anyone look good on the dance floor" which was – and still is – true. "Just follow my lead."

Most of the dancing was simply good fun, but with some women, the dancing was taken to a whole new level. My absolute favorite thing was when a woman's hips would meet mine. It only happened once or twice and I'll never forget the first time it happened. I was dancing with a gorgeous woman named Bella who was far taller than most girls our age. She was nearly my height at the time and an excellent dancer, so her hips were in perfect sync with mine, as if we were fused together. It was such a perfect moment for me that I have reflected on it often throughout the years, wondering who she was and what happened to her. That night, when we left the bar, I went on and on telling Lou about how magical the dancing with her was and said, "That kind of thing only happens once in a lifetime."

Sometimes, as a teen, I would get overly excited while dancing. So excited, in fact, that I'd climax. And this was in a time when dancing typically had far less contact than nowadays. I experienced a similar situation in gym class, at around twelve, when we went rope climbing. I didn't know what the hell had happened – all I knew was boy, it felt good and left me thinking: I want to climb that rope all the time. I didn't tell any of my friends about that story, though, probably because I had no idea how to even describe it.

Fortunately, no one really knew about the issue I had dancing with girls either – at least not until I told Lou because I wanted to know if it happened to him too. He started laughing hysterically at me and needless to say, he did not have the same issue. It became the butt of many jokes between us. "You love women so much you orgasm just holdin' 'em," he cracked.

During my senior year of high school, I got a job at a nearby factory in Wallington, which was the Polish neighborhood next to Garfield. I think I was the only guy in there who wasn't Polish or Russian, but they welcomed me in as the lone Italian.

The factory made electrical transformers and my job was to cart these transformers around different parts of the factory. Because I pushed these huge transformers around all day, my buddy Joe Bosco started nicknaming me "The Truck." After a day's work in the factory we'd wash up in a communal area, because we were all covered in grime. There were many times I looked at the older guys toiling away in the factory and I thought about how hard it would be to work this job day in and day out for decades.

Shortly before I graduated, I was offered a position "upstairs," or in entry-level management at the factory, but I didn't consider it – I told them I was going to college. Sure, I would have had a steady income if I took the job, but I thought of all the older Polish guys and knew I didn't want to plod my way to the factory with a salami sandwich for the rest of my life. I also knew I wanted to be a doctor and college was the next necessary step to reaching my goal.

My friend Lou was at Clarkson University, which was a great engineering school. I didn't have the grades or the money to go to a university like that, but I applied to different schools that were more in my reach, including a couple of junior colleges.

When I was accepted to two of the junior colleges I applied to, I was relieved and elated, even though one of those acceptances was conditional. Given where I was in life, I was so thrilled with this result that I went around bragging that I was accepted to a junior college – on probation. Back then, I had never even heard of an Ivy League school; I was simply thrilled to be going to Farleigh Dickinson, a junior college a couple of towns away.

The guys I worked with at the factory congratulated me on my acceptance and I could see the pride some of them had in their eyes as they wished me well. They were truly happy that I was taking a different path and bettering myself.

My last day on the job, some of my Polish buddies at the factory invited me to play a game of poker. I knew the basics of the game, but they were experts. Surprisingly, I kept getting good hands. It got to my head and I started thinking, "I'm gonna wipe these guys out," and eventually, I did – I got a royal flush and was on my way with a little wad of cash. At the time, I thought I had just been incredibly lucky. When I looked back on it years later, I realized my industrious coworkers knew I was broke and going off to college and wanted to help out a hardworking kid. I admire their generosity and have to chuckle at my innocence, thinking I was winning hand after hand, even landing a royal flush.

Cleaning up after a day of working at the factory

CHAPTER 6

Conditional Acceptance

SITTING ON THE BALCONY OVERLOOKING the large, immaculate grounds of my college, I imagined I was in England. After all, the school was built like a castle and I was taking a class in English literature. Despite being a kid from the streets, I found myself at Farleigh Dickinson University, which was a place of unprecedented culture in my eyes. Although back then, it wasn't a university yet; it was a two-year college.

It sure looked like a university, though. I imagine the campus – especially in the wintertime, covered in snow – rivaled some of the top schools. Farleigh Dickinson was in Rutherford at the time, which is a town close to Garfield.

Fairleigh Dickinson, 1950

I never grew tired of the campus – meaning I never took it for granted. There actually was a building molded after a French castle that sat in the middle of the campus. The huge lawn that I loved to view from the castle balcony was worlds away from the streets. I was with rich people. Well, relatively rich people, compared to me. College was a whole new life for me. I never dreamed of such a life. Farleigh was a refuge and a stunning scene. Being in this beautiful educational environment fueled my curiosity; more then ever I wanted to understand the intricacies of the human body and discover what else the world had to offer.

This new environment had quite different standards than anywhere I had spent time before. Every day at school, all the men had to dress in a sports coat and tie, as our president wanted to make sure we maintained a certain level of propriety and class. This was 1949, and the idea was that we would be business leaders of the future, so we should look and act the part.

Although I looked the part, all cleaned up for class, I was still myself. You can take the kid out of the street, but you can't always take the street out of the kid. To this day, some friends tell me, "Joe, you're too much yourself." There are certain elements of who I am that stay fixed, and one of them is stubbornness in my approach to problem solving.

Early on in my chemistry class, the kind professor asked for a volunteer to solve a problem. I raised my hand and she chose me, so I started working it out on the chalkboard. I looked over at her, hoping to see some approval, but instead found a quizzical look on her face, as though she didn't know whether or not my solution was right.

"That's incorrect," a fellow student said from the back of the class. I felt a surge of anger well up. I had put the problem up proudly, but my cheeks were burning when I heard my classmate's objection. I did things my way, like Sinatra said – I had to solve problems my way. And although my approach was unorthodox in this situation, I was pretty confident I had the right solution.

"Whadya mean it's wrong?" I yelled. "I'll smack you in the face!" I hadn't thought about what I was saying; it just came out that way. That's how I would have talked to my gang in high school. And they would have hollered back just as colorfully.

Fortunately, the professor was a charming and wonderful woman, in addition to being a good teacher, and gently told me the error in my way.

She cleared her throat and simply said, "Now Joseph, here in college if we disagree with someone, we just disagree and say why." It was as if she were giving me an etiquette lesson, in a nice way.

As time went by, I learned to have more of a sense of decorum in the classroom, at least to some degree. I would often ask questions and raise my hand to share my thoughts. In my English literature class, I was bombarded by many vocabulary words I didn't know. Wanting to learn more, I would actually stop the professor in the middle of class every time he used a word that was new to me. People would laugh, but I didn't care; I didn't know what one-upmanship meant.

My class in English literature surprised me – I had never enjoyed fiction before. Since I was small, I loved to read, but I had almost exclusively read science books. It was interesting to find myself immersed in something entirely different, like *Sir Gawain and the Green Knight* and *My Last Duchess*. Reading these works, I was taken away to a sort of fantasyland, especially when I found myself sitting on the castle balcony, looking out at the campus and imagining I was some place across the pond.

Although my courses interested me, I loved to joke around in class, even with the teachers. Many people don't know how to pronounce my last name, but they generally pronounce it one of two ways: "Tur-sill-oh" or "Tur-see-loh." The first one is correct, as far as I'm concerned. Regardless, however a professor would pronounce my name, I would stop her and say it was actually pronounced the other way.

After the first two months or so of school, I dialed back on the jokes and started buckling down on my studies. I chose to go into being a lab technician my first and second year of college. I didn't dare go into pre-med (but that wasn't even an option, because they didn't have a pre-med track at my two-year college). At that time, although I knew I wanted to be a doctor, I thought to myself: What the hell do I know? So I settled for the lab technician major. At least that would take me in the direction of a hospital setting.

When I first started at Farleigh, I lived with my mom at our flat on 45 Harrison Ave. At the end of the school day, I would walk away from the beautiful campus and take two busses back to our flat, which I still called home. When I got home, my mom would usually be cooking and we'd have dinner together.

But there were many days where, after class, I would sit on that balcony and daydream about being in a distant country. I took in the sunlight, shut my eyes, and wondered what was out there. New York was the furthest I had ventured from home.

I recall trying to smoke out on that balcony, wanting to look like Joe Cool with the pipe. But I never really got into it, because you had to carry this large pipe around and I'd either forget the pipe or the tobacco and one without the other was of course useless.

Later on, cigarettes seemed to be the thing to have. So I bought a pack but found that I couldn't really inhale properly, no matter how much I tried. Then I'd always forget to buy more cigarettes and when I did remember, I didn't know where to keep them (In my back pocket? In my front pocket?) After a while, I just admitted I wasn't that interested in smoking and gave it up.

During my first year, I was excited to get a call from my Uncle Willy, who lived a few towns away from us in Patterson. I loved my Uncle Willy – he looked like a stereotypical gangster, with his suit, potbelly, and a cigar dangling from his mouth as he drove around in his Cadillac. But he wasn't a gangster at all – he was actually a union man. It was unusual for me to hear from him, though, as he traveled a great deal for business.

Uncle Willy did pretty well for himself and had a nice home. His wife, my Aunt Angie, was not the warmest woman, but she was kind enough and took care of the affairs in the house. By that, I mean that she spent most of her time decorating.

Uncle Willy called because he said that he was traveling a lot for work and my Aunt Angie needed someone to drive her around. He asked if I wanted to come live with them and drive my aunt in exchange for a place to stay. I thought about their house – palatial compared to my mom's flat, plus it had hot water and ample electricity – and figured it would be nice to live in that sort of luxury for a while.

I spoke with my mom about it and she approved; she wanted me to be in a place where she knew I'd be fed well. I was accustomed, for various reasons – whether it was my mom being fed up with being a single parent, or money being too tight, or bad behavior as a child – to living with other family members for periods of time.

When I arrived in their house with my bags and was shown to my room, I went into the bathroom to freshen up. I turned on the hot water and was in awe of how easily hot water flowed out of the faucet. How much time they must save, I thought, by being able to skip the daily task of heating water up on a stove every time they wanted to bathe or cook.

Uncle Willy took me under his wing, wanting to make sure I was educated in ways that an Italian father was expected to teach his son. He took me to nice Italian restaurants in New York so I could learn about dining at fancier places. I'll never forget one of the first times we went and I was silent, staring around at the nice restaurant with waiters in tuxes. Uncle Willy stared at me with a bit of a grimace on his face, as if waiting for me to say something, but I was speechless, just drinking my cappuccino.

"'Ey, don't be dumb," Uncle Willy said in his thick accent, with his cigar in hand, snapping me out of my reverie. "Why don't you say, 'What a nice place you have here, Sir'?" Ever since then, I always try to compliment a waiter or owner on their restaurant – especially if it's an Italian establishment.

The best part of living with Uncle Willy and Aunt Angie was the cars. Even while I was chauffeuring my aunt around in the Cadillac and Hudson, I was in my glory, driving those huge cars around. It was quite a step up from my own car, the one I had to start with a hammer.

Aunt Angie and I had an amicable relationship, but it was nothing like the closeness I had with Uncle Willy. I mostly just drove her around and engaged in small talk. This was usually pleasant enough, but sometimes I grew tired of her unsolicited advice. At one point, she caught wind of my life ambition – to become a doctor. She seemed surprised to hear this and bluntly said, "You'll never be a doctor. You don't know anyone and you don't have any money."

I don't think I said anything in reply but fortunately, I didn't take her comment seriously or personally. Perhaps I was too naïve. The odds were pretty much all against me, but I was too innocent and optimistic to realize it. As far as I was concerned, the only way to go was up.

Driving Angie around in the luxury cars was all good and fun until one day my uncle received a notice that I was due in court for outrunning a police officer. Uncle Willy was shocked but perfectly calm when he approached me with the ticket.

"Joe, what is this?" he asked, handing me the ticket. I looked it over in confusion and truly had no idea what the ticket was regarding. Although I did like getting up to some trouble, I never would have tried to evade a cop.

"Did you really do that?" he asked.

"Outrun a cop? Are you crazy?" I retorted. "Of course not! I have no idea what this is," I said nervously. I had never been in court before. The notice said I had been in the Hudson, which was a supercharged car. When I found out more information in court, I learned that the cop who tried to pull me over had been on a motorcycle, so I figured he probably had been too slow and small for me to even notice him behind me.

The day before I was due in court, my uncle told me to meet him at a warehouse. Though I was confused and a bit nervous, I quickly obeyed and went to the address he gave me. Once there, I waited for him as he briefly spoke with a couple of men on the other end of the warehouse. Then he walked toward me, in his usual garb, looking like a gangster. He gestured his head toward the door and we left. It was clear Uncle Willy was up to something; I had no idea what was going on or why I had to go to a random warehouse, but I didn't ask any questions.

The next day, I found myself in court with a lawyer standing next to me. I had no idea how I even got the lawyer, as I did nothing to arrange for one; the man just appeared. Things moved quickly from there. The lawyer represented me and the case was swiftly dismissed. I wondered how it all resolved so effortlessly, but wasn't going to linger around and wonder why – I was just thrilled to be off the hook. As I walked out, the sheriff who took notes during the trial stopped me and said, "Boy, you're a lucky guy. The last kid who did this was sent to prison." I was shocked but continued on my way, as if they might change their mind if I hesitated.

I never asked my uncle about his involvement in resolving the case, but I assume he was behind the scenes working things out for me, like the god-father. Uncle Willy always stood by me. He never hit me, never hollered at me – he just stood by me.

Just as I had in high school, I tried to experience as much as I could in college. I joined the track and field team, became one of the Farleigh Knights (which was a group of us who got to dress up as our mascot, on occasion), went to every party I could, dated every pretty girl I could, and most importantly, studied my ass off.

My closest friends in college were Horace, my childhood friend, and some new buddies named Fred and Frank. I was fortunate to have friends like Frank – he was the most honorable guy you could want to meet. He was the Gregory Peck of the college, as far as I was concerned. His father was a big shot industrialist and he was serious about his studies.

Fred was also a good student and an honorable young man. We spent a lot of time together, just roaming around campus, going to parties, and studying. One day we were walking to class and Fred pointed out a beautiful brand new Buick. I stopped another student walking by and asked him to take a picture of us in front of it, as if it were my car. Later on, we got a good laugh when that picture appeared in the yearbook with the caption "Playboys."

Every year the school had a production called Farleigh Follies, which was like a vaudeville show involving comedy, dance, and other short acts. One year, I volunteered to be student director of the show, so I was the MC and did a comedy act with Horace. I loved being on stage, just as I had in high school, and felt elated with the audience cheering us on and laughing at our act. It was also a fun task to choose who would be in the show and evaluate all the other students as they tried out.

College was full of far more festivities than I could have imagined. Our Halloween celebrations were delightful because we always had a party in the castle, which created a spectacular – and with the Halloween decorations – spooky ambiance. One year I dressed in a cap and gown and wore a sign around my neck that read "Not your ordinary high school graduate."

Then there were the dances. I loved those affairs, dressing up and dancing around with my date. Our junior prom was the most memorable because I took a beautiful girl who happened to have the sexiest dress of anyone there. She had a strapless dress, and back then, to have your shoulders showing was quite risqué.

Toward the end of my second year at Farleigh, we found out the school was going to become a four-year university. I didn't think about it that much at the time, but upon reflection I realize how impeccable my timing was – I was able to seamlessly extend my studies into the four-year bachelor's degree. I was thrilled about this opportunity, and by that time, I was confident enough in my abilities to apply for pre-med. I ended up pursuing majors in biology and psychology. I went to two summer sessions, trying to gain as many credits as I could – hoping that would give me an edge when I applied to med schools.

Once Uncle Willy knew I was studying medicine, he was quite proud of my choice and said, "Don't you ever give up medicine, Joey. Don't ever give that up." He only said it once, but that was all I needed to hear it. I wasn't going to give up anyway; as far as I was concerned, there was no place else to go. If I didn't become a doctor, I didn't know what I would do. But I admired Uncle Willy and appreciated his belief in my chosen profession.

After becoming a pre-med student, I became even more diligent in my studies. The courses were, of course, notably more challenging than the previous two years, but they were also far more interesting. As usual, I enjoyed reading my science books and learning more about how to diagnose and heal human ailments.

I got closer to my friend Frank when I took organic chemistry, because he helped me out with the class. As I look back on it, I realize I had a lot of people help me; things like organic chemistry and German were like Chinese to me. I also did my best to help my friends out where I could.

Continuing on my way, taking each course step by step, I made it to graduation. I was the first kid in my family to graduate from college and my mom was incredibly proud of me. That said, I unfortunately did not get into medical school right out of college. I remained undeterred though, whether it was by stubbornness, optimism, or ignorance, I can't say for sure; it was probably some combination of them all.

That summer after graduating Farleigh Dickinson, I sought out a job at a local hospital to get more experience in the medical field and to earn some money. Passaic General Hospital took me in as a guy who would clean up after surgery. This essentially entailed going into the operating room after surgery and mopping up large amounts of blood off the floor, then taking the bloody sheets and washing as much blood off of them as possible before throwing them down the laundry shoot. Fortunately, I've never been bothered by the sight of blood. Perhaps it's the Sicilian background.

Although this was work that required no medical knowledge, I was happy to do it. Looking back on it, I don't think any of us are above certain types of jobs. And at the time, I certainly didn't think I was above mopping the floors. On the contrary, I was just glad to be working in a hospital and getting some exposure to doctors, even if it was only in passing.

CHAPTER 7

Lorelei

———

WHILE OUR HIGH SCHOOL DAYS involved weekly visits to Club Nolan, we expanded our horizons in college. Our new Friday night adventure typically took us into New York, at a German nightclub called Lorelei's on 86ᵗʰ St. This club had the most beautiful girls, many of whom were European immigrants. When I walked into Lorelei's, I felt like a kid in a candy store.

Dressed up for a night out

Usually Lou drove on our Friday night expeditions, but occasionally I took the General out. The car that Horace gave me (well, sold me, though I still hadn't paid him) at sixteen was sometimes still able to run. I didn't typically take it far distances because it broke down so much. But I wasn't worried about that on this particular night because Horace was on board and could troubleshoot in case something went wrong. After starting the car with a hammer as usual, Horace, Lou, and I were on our way to Lorelei's, talking and laughing. It was a peaceful drive along certain stretches, especially along the shore.

As we drove through the quaint New York town of Poughkeepsie, taking in the sea breeze on a warm night, I glanced at my rearview mirror and noticed a small stream of smoke wafting from underneath the back of my car.

"Shit," I muttered. I nudged Horace, who was sitting shotgun, and pointed at the mirror. "Horace, what's going on? There's smoke."

"Pull over!" Horace yelled. I pressed the brakes and pulled over. "Get out of the car," Horace demanded as soon as the car was stopped. Horace was typically a mellow guy. Judging by his frazzled reaction, I suspected that my car was a goner.

We all piled out and ran off as we noticed the smoke steadily increasing. Soon it was billowing into a dark cloud, slowly rising toward the night sky. Horace had his hands on each side of his face. Although it was my car, I actually still hadn't paid him for it and he was the one who took pride in it. After each breakdown, Horace was the one to fix it up. Besides, I still owed him twenty bucks for it.

I looked on in concern. Suddenly there was a spark and we could see fire start to overtake the entire car. We backed away, onto the sand and watched as the General was engulfed in flames. Lou and I just stood there silently while Horace let out some audible sounds of distress.

"What are we gonna do now?" I asked Lou. Calm as ever, Lou shrugged and looked around.

"Well we gotta make a friend and use their phone," he replied. "Hey, Horace! The car's gone. Sorry, buddy. Let's go get some help." Horace slowly walked over with his chin down.

We walked along the sidewalk of the sleepy town and wondered who we'd ask for help. After a few minutes, I saw a few girls walking along the sand up ahead and proceeded toward them. As we got closer, it seemed the girls were a little surprised to see a few guys approaching them late at night, so I began to quickly explain our predicament.

"Hey there, can I ask you a favor?" I asked the girl in front.

"What's that?" she asked timidly.

"My car just burned down," I said, pointing back toward what remained of the General. It was still billowing with smoke, so the girls clearly believed us.

"Oh my," she replied, her brow furrowing in concern.

"We need to call someone to pick us up. Do any of you live nearby and have a phone we could use?" I asked.

One of the girls lived nearby and told us we could stop by quickly to make a call. As we meandered down the streets, I got to talking to the girl I initially approached, whose name was Linda. The two of us hit it off to a degree and she started talking to me about books that she loved. They were all books I had never heard of.

"You've never heard of *The Catcher in the Rye*?" she asked, surprised.

"No. I don't read novels."

"What do you read?"

"Science books. I love to learn about chemistry and biology."

"Really?" she replied, now truly surprised.

"Yeah. Science is fascinating."

Lou came back inside after calling one of his brothers.

"My brother will pick us up in the morning," he said. "We'll have to figure out where to stay until then," Lou said.

The girls weren't gonna have a bunch of strangers sleep over but pointed us in the direction of the police department to report the car incident and ask them where we could go. Before I left, Linda pulled me aside and opened her purse.

"Here, I want you to have this," she said, placing a book in my hand. It was *The Catcher in the Rye*. "I just finished it. I'm sure you'll love it. All the college kids do."

Once we got to the police station, we told the cops what had happened and they seemed somewhat relieved to see that we escaped the burning car unscathed.

"My brother is picking us up in the morning, but we don't have anywhere to go tonight," Lou said.

"There are some local hotels but if you don't have any money, the only other place to stay is the jail," the policeman said. We shrugged.

"Jail it is, I suppose," Lou said.

It was incredibly strange, to willingly walk into a jail cell, knowing you'd just spend the night. At this point, I was so tired, I didn't really care. They put us in a cell with a few cots, fortunately without any other inmates, and we went to bed. In the morning I woke up early to the natural light and the springs of the thin, old mattress jutting into my back. Horace and Lou were still asleep, so I pulled out my book and started reading about Holden Caulfield.

Not much reading time went by before Lou's brother arrived and we left the jail. When I finally made it back home, I washed up and told my mom the car burned down. I left out the part about where we spent the night. Once I was cleaned up, I went back to reading *The Catcher in the Rye*. It was the first novel I ever enjoyed and still one of the few I've ever read. I recall feeling very sophisticated reading it, since I knew it was popular among many college kids and a bit controversial. Regardless of its popularity, I could identify with the loneliness that the narrator felt. Of course, I was a very social guy, but because of my childhood, there was often a lingering feeling of loneliness, or at least a lingering fear of solitude.

Although my car was gone, we continued our adventures into the city unde-terred. When we went out, it was often just Lou, Horace, and me but some-times we brought chicks along with us. Having group dates was fun so once Lou and I asked the two girls we were taking out to set our buddy Al up with another girl. Al was a friend of Lou's at Clarkson and was visiting, so he didn't really know anyone in town. We figured he wouldn't be a tough sell – he was attractive, intelligent, and humorous. My date agreed to set Al up with one of her friends. She told us to pick up her friend, Carrie, at the Astor Hotel the following night.

A group of us pulled up to the Astor, as directed, and saw a homely young woman waiting on the curb with a huge smile on her face. For a second, I hoped that wasn't the girl Al was supposed to go out with, but my date started waving at her and rolled down the window and spoke to her. I looked over at Al and saw a look of complete shock on his face.

It took a lot of willpower to contain myself from laughing when I saw Al's frozen smile and colorless countenance as he introduced himself to Carrie, who was delighted when she saw Al. I looked at Lou and Al and could tell Lou was also trying to suppress his amusement.

"Well, where to?" Lou asked cheerfully. And with that, Al was stuck with this date for the night. And it would be a long night for him, considering Lou and I were pleased with our dates and weren't planning on ending the night anytime early. After going to a bar or two, we wandered around wondering what to do next.

I suggested we go to my dad's, which was an unusual occurrence, but at this time he was living with one of my uncles and things were pretty stable for him, so I occasionally dropped by to visit. Going out in New York was fun, but very expensive. Going to my uncle's house in New Jersey was free.

My dad was always paranoid about people trying to get him; even if he had the means to buy his own place, he probably wouldn't have. We pulled up to my uncle's house and let ourselves in.

After making ourselves at home on the couch, we poured ourselves some drinks and started talking. My father came out after a while and said hello. I noticed him give a quizzical look as he scanned the room and saw Carrie. When Lou and I got up to grab some more drinks, my dad pulled us aside and lowered his voice to ask, "'Ey, what cage did you get this animal from?" From his tone, it was clear he was completely serious and didn't see anything wrong with asking a question of this nature.

Lou and I were silent for a second, in slight shock, then we burst out laughing, unable to contain ourselves any longer. Al, Carrie and the other girls looked over at us a second but didn't know what we were amused about, so they continued on with their discussion. I explained to my dad that it was a blind date and we hadn't known who this girl was or what she looked like. He mumbled something about making a better choice next time and poured himself a drink.

Poor Al had to endure another few hours of entertaining a girl he had zero interest in while the rest of us, probably even Carrie, had a good time. When we finally dropped her and the other girls off, Lou and I started laughing hysterically at Al.

"Was that on purpose?" Al asked us.

"No! We wouldn't do that!" we insisted. "We had no idea who that girl was! Her friend was sure pretty, though" I added, referring to the girl I had taken out.

Al sighed and retorted, "I'm never letting you guys set me up again."

In retrospect, I realize we shouldn't have said such things about Carrie or judged her based on her looks. In particular, I can only hope God forgives my father and me for his statement. But that's the kind of guy my dad was. He didn't mean any harm, but he said exactly what was on his mind – and he seemed to lack any barometer for sensitivity. Nights like those, when friends and I stopped by and saw my dad, were quite rare. He kept moving from place to place and I often didn't even know where he was. Eventually, he decided to leave the country altogether and moved to Trinidad, in the Caribbean. Once he became an ex-pat, we hardly ever communicated; many years would go by without us speaking at all. Both of us were bad about writing letters and I didn't particularly get the sense that he was eager to hear from me, though I would have loved if that weren't the case.

CHAPTER 8

Midwestern Schooling

I WAS AS SURPRISED AS anyone else to find myself in St. Louis for graduate school. Initially I wanted to go to medical school in or near New Jersey, but there were two problems with that plan. First, there were no medical schools in the state at that time. Second, the medical schools I did apply to didn't accept me straight out of college. I figured there wasn't much point in continuously applying and looked at other graduate programs in science instead.

St. Louis University accepted me for virtually every master's program they had in science. I ended up choosing biophysics. My plan was to study at St. Louis for two or three years, learn as much as I could, then apply to more medical schools. I chose St. Louis because it was a Jesuit school and I wanted to learn more about my religion.

Before my arrival, I had arranged to live with a group of guys I had never met. Fortunately, they turned out to be a group of kind Midwestern boys with good values. We lived in a house on Vandaveda Street and ended up calling ourselves the Vandaveda Vandals. I was the only one of them who wasn't from the Midwest. The guys got a kick out of my Jersey accent and loved to hear stories about what life was like in Garfield. It was all chummy.

The Midwest was quite a change from Jersey. I went from living in a cluster of East Coast Italian families to being surrounded by Midwesterners. The pace of life was slower in St. Louis just about everywhere, except on campus. The youthful energy of the university and the intense academic mindset of the professors made the campus a pleasantly busy place.

Shortly after my arrival, I applied for a research position with the pharmacology department, and somehow got the job. I remember being surprised at my acceptance because I knew many of the other applicants were more refined and had been to more prestigious undergraduate schools. I worked under a brilliant Japanese professor, Kazi Kamura, who had both a Ph.D and an MD. I enjoyed this job and continued immersing myself in coursework. In my free time, I'd get to know the guys I lived with and we'd occasionally go over to the nearby women's colleges to meet girls.

Every year, there would be a dance to introduce the students at the girls' colleges to the St. Louis students (our student body was nearly all men at the time). The dance was called Icebreaker and all the guys got very excited to meet the new girls. "Hey-ayy-ayy, we're goin' to see the girls!" I'd say to my housemates as we got ready.

As always, I was delighted to go to a dance. I got to show off my moves and meet a lot of girls – although we could never get too close. On each end of the dance floor, there were nuns watching us like hawks, making sure there was ample space between the men and the women as we danced.

While my weekdays were packed full with studying and work, my weekends were mostly spent with my buddies. On a typical weekend afternoon, my friend Joe Medeski and I were walking down the main street in our Sunday best. We didn't have any money to spend, but were looking to entertain ourselves. Joe was a dental student and lived in the Vandaveda house. There was an unusual amount of activity this Sunday, perhaps because the weather was unusually nice. Many families were out after church and other students were socializing as well.

As we passed one of the local hotels, we noticed a group of well-dressed middle-aged people congregating for some sort of event. Joe and I took interest and peered in to see what was going on: There was a reception desk where people were checking in and a sign that read "Welcome, new members of City of Hope." We didn't really have anything else to do, so I figured maybe we should join the party. I looked at Joe and Joe looked at me, and without saying a word, we both put our shoulders back and strutted in past the reception desk, as if we were longtime members.

We walked in to find immaculately set tables with different types of whiskey for the taking. Joe and I sat down and promptly began pouring a drink. I lifted up my glass and said, "Joe, I'd like to make a toast...to the City of Hope, whatever that may be." Joe and I stifled our laughter and wondered what we had gotten ourselves into. After taking a sip, Joe looked at me in slight shock.

"What is this?" he asked. "I've never tasted such delightful whiskey..." I nodded in agreement. I also had never had such a smooth drink.

"Must be nice to be rich," I joked as I took another swig of my drink.

Fortunately, the MC started making announcements before other new members could get a chance to talk to us and discover that we actually had no idea what this event was for.

"We are so pleased to welcome our new members to City of Hope..." the MC announced. He proceeded to talk about what value City of Hope was bringing as a non-profit research institution and hospital. Joe and I politely listened and played the part of interested new members as we continued enjoying our fine liquor.

"And now, will all our new members please stand up," the MC said exuberantly. I took a gulp of my drink and looked over at Joe, and he looked at me. Silently, we nodded at each other and stood up. The room of about 100 people had a decent amount of new members, and we accepted the welcoming applause with polite smiles. I had never heard of City of Hope until that day.

Once the event seemed to be winding down, we snuck out and continued idling down the street. A few blocks down the road, we burst out laughing, feeling our whiskey and joking on and on about our drunken farce. At the time, I had no idea that I would eventually join City of Hope and become a proud advocate of the organization.

CHAPTER 9

Scrubbing In

I PLANNED TO RETURN TO Passaic General Hospital after my first year at St. Louis University to mop the floors for another summer. Shortly after my arrival, I began the same old job – prepping the OR and cleaning the bloody mess that was left after surgery. Although it was routine, I was happy to find myself in the hospital atmosphere and to expose myself to so many doctors, even if I only saw them in passing.

Not very far in to the summer, my supervisor told me I was being promoted. Promoted! I thought. How wonderful. I never would have guessed what that advancement would be, but they told me I was being promoted to a scrub nurse.

Going from mopping floors to assisting doctors in surgery was quite a leap. They could have hired an RN, but that would have cost far more, so they hired me to save money. After all my experience prepping and cleaning the operating room, they knew I could be trained as a scrub nurse fairly quickly. I jumped at the opportunity to scrub in and assist in surgery. Getting to see the doctors operate was a wonder to me, given all the years I had dreamed of being a doctor.

Every morning, as I scrubbed in, I would wash my hands at the sink and put on my face mask. I'd look at myself in the mirror for a few seconds and tell myself, "One day, I'm going to be a doctor." Then I'd head in to surgery.

The work in the hospital was always high energy, as the stakes are high in an operation. As the saying goes, there are no minor surgeries, only minor surgeons. Fortunately, the doctors I shadowed were incredible surgeons. But that's not to say they were always pleasant to work for. One doctor in particular, Dr. O'Malley, was dubbed "the urological surgeon of terror." Fortunately, I didn't know that when I went into surgery with him one day. If I had, I may have been nervous, as the other nurses were. But I didn't know anything about his reputation at this point, so I didn't know any better. Sometimes, not knowing any better helps you.

In this particular surgery, the patient had so much bleeding in the prostate that the doctor couldn't control the bleeding. I didn't know what the hell was going on, but I used my best judgment as I handed Dr. O'Malley the instruments that I thought would be most appropriate. In the end, everything was fine and the surgery was successful. Dr. O'Malley told me he appreciated my aggressiveness in handing him the proper instruments. And from that point on, he only wanted me assisting him.

As I got more proficient in the operating room, some of the doctors started to let me sew up after surgery. I learned to suture quite quickly and enjoyed doing it. When I was sewing up, it almost felt like I was a doctor.

The scrub nurse job involved a very early wakeup call. Every morning I was up at five-thirty. While I loved working in surgery and being surrounded by doctors, I quickly questioned whether or not I wanted to be a surgeon. I imagined myself waking up so early every day, exhausted, then standing working on patients for countless hours. I knew that if I tried doing that until I was sixty, I would be completely worn out. At this point, I still was unsure what kind of doctor I wanted to be, but I felt I did not have the physical stamina to be a surgeon – or at least I did not want to wake up well before the crack of dawn every morning.

I had always been fascinated by the science of the body and figuring out complex cases. Eventually this helped me realize I should be an internist. And as I got older, I could study in a chair, instead of standing for hours on end operating. Moreover, if I was an internist, I could prevent many surgeries by spotting problems early on and encouraging my patients to become healthier.

I got to know the staff at Passaic General quite well over the years, as I ended up working there four summers. My second to last summer, a certain nurse caught my eye. She was a kind Polish girl named Dolores. We began to date and I asked her to go steady with me after a while. The way I felt about Dolores was different from the other girls; I actually felt I might have a future with her.

When I brought her over to meet my mother, they had an instant liking for one another. Being a nurse, Dolores was a sensitive and caring person. My mom was naturally warm and took on the role of caring for others, so I suppose they understood each other in that regard. Over dinner, we were all surprised to find that my mom had been friends with Dolores' mom – they had worked in the same factory for years. We all laughed at the coincidence and I saw a gleam in my mom's eye when she looked at the two of us.

With Dolores, I didn't think about other girls as much. However, one day I was forced to. I was scrubbed in and walked over to the patient lying on the table, who was being prepped for surgery. She looked at me with a sense of disbelief. Before she said anything, I recognized her.

"Joe!" she practically yelled.

"Jean?" I asked, puzzled. What was she doing here? I thought. She was a young girl, my age. I had seen her chart and before she told me anything, I knew why she was there: colon cancer, which was very hard to treat in those days. I looked at her and couldn't believe that my first serious girlfriend was lying before me on an operating table.

We exchanged a few words and then had to proceed with the next steps for surgery. Her surgery went fine and Dolores and I went to visit her in recovery. I had never run in to anyone I had known in the hospital, so I couldn't believe the coincidence of running into one of the first girls I loved in the operating room. After returning to St. Louis for the fall, seeing Jean seemed almost like a distant dream, a hazy but persistent memory.

The first year at St. Louis was wonderful, but the second year was my formative time at the university. One of my favorite classes that year was a biophysics class with Father Basile Luyet, who was an eminent scientist from Switzerland. He was a rather famous scientist at the time and is considered the father of cryobiology, which is a branch of biology that studies how living things are affected by low temperatures. Father Luyet was brilliant. After a few days in his class a position in his lab opened up. I didn't think I had much of a chance at getting the job, but I figured it wouldn't hurt to apply. Once I got an interview, I was thrilled, although I still remained cautiously optimistic about my actual chances of being chosen for the position.

The day after my interview, I arrived early to class and started reviewing my notes. A few moments later, Father Luyet came in and said, "Morning, Joseph." Then he got to work writing out his lesson on the board. Father wasn't one for small talk; he was straight to business. After a few minutes of furiously writing on the chalkboard, he grabbed an envelope from his desk and walked over to me.

"This is for you," he said as he handed it to me. Without waiting for any reply, he swiftly turned around and returned to his rapid writing. I looked down at the envelope, wondering what it was.

I opened the letter as students trickled in, talking excitedly about the weekend ahead. A signature at the bottom caught my eye; it was signed by a nun named Sister Mary Pierre. I wondered who that was. I scanned the top to read that she was Luyet's head researcher and that she looked forward to working with me. I had a big smile on my face as class started and I knew I would have the opportunity to work directly with Father.

Most of my second year at St. Louis was spent in Father Luyet's lab. On my first day, I was introduced to Sister Mary Pierre. Sister Mary was not your typical nun. Hailing from Germany, she was also a researcher with a Ph.D. She served as Father Luyet's right hand man. On top of her intelligence, she was an incredibly attractive woman with the most caring soul.

Sister was a savior to me. For one thing, she served as an intermediary between Father Luyet and me. Father was so intelligent and esoteric that, although he spoke fluent English, it often seemed like he was speaking in another tongue. I think he also was sometimes thrown off by my thick Jersey accent and slang. Fortunately, Sister Mary was able to translate what we meant to each other in times where one or both of us were confused.

I am not sure why, but Sister took me in and looked after me. She must have known I was a rascal who needed to be straightened out. I think she also found me amusing and enjoyed spending time together. Being taken under her wing was a blessing. Sister would bring me food from the convent and nurture me; she became like a mother to me. In appreciation for her guidance and generosity, I committed to being more religious, wanting to make her proud. I started going to Church every Sunday and after a while, I was going to Mass every morning – at 6 am. I went simply because Sister wanted me to go. And I'm glad I did, because it taught me lessons in morality that I didn't learn growing up with my gang in Jersey.

Sister Mary

As a kid, I rarely went to church with my family. However, I do remember one of the first times I went to confession, when I was a child. I was afraid to go in before the priest and tell him all my terrible sins – at age seven. I was shit scared to confess to the priest, though I laugh at myself now, because I no longer know what those "sins" were. Maybe I felt sinful for thinking about sex, but for all I know, the sins were imaginary. In my days at St. Louis, I found Mass decently enjoyable and occasionally went to confession, which was usually refreshing.

While I learned more about faith from Sister, I learned a great deal of discipline from Father. I was astounded when I first learned about his routine and work ethic. Believing the morning hours were the best time for reflection and clear thinking, Father woke at 3:00 am and meditated until 6:00 am. He then said Mass daily at 6:00 am at St. Margaret's Catholic Church. Next he went to the lab at 7:00 am and worked until 8:00 pm. He did not retire until 9:30 pm.

Given his work ethic, Father expected a lot from me as well. He often had me working in the lab until one or two in the morning, even on some Friday and Saturday nights. I kept working away, thankful that I had a good job and two wonderful mentors.

CHAPTER 10

Icebreaker

AFTER SETTLING IN TO MY new job and the new school year, it was time for another Icebreaker dance with the girls. I put on my suit, tie, and dancing shoes before meeting up with my buddy Tom to walk over to the girl's college.

The dance was more festive this year than last and they quickly announced there would be a dance contest later in the night.

"Ya hear that, Tom?" I said as I clapped him on the shoulder. "A dance contest!"

"Bet you think you're gonna win, huh?" Tom said playfully. I looked around and didn't see any other guy who was an incredibly good dancer.

"Looks like I have a shot," I said with a grin. "Let's hit the dance floor!"

After a couple of hours of dancing and socializing with the girls, one of the students announced the dance contest was about to begin. They said there would be one winner, which surprised me – I had expected there to be a male and female winner. I wasn't after the prize, because I didn't know what it would be, but I obviously wanted to win so that more girls would notice me. I danced with different girls in the contest, mostly doing the jitterbug. When a Sinatra song came on, I was on cloud nine as I danced with a particularly beautiful girl, dipping her and spinning her in syncopation with the smooth, familiar beat.

When the song stopped, everyone began clapping and a student got on stage. "Alright, we have a winner!" she announced. "Drumroll, please," she said slowly. I looked around as the female students knowingly began doing the drumroll on their thighs and the males quickly followed suit. "And the winner is...Joseph Turcillo!" There was a loud applause and I had to catch my breath from all the dancing. "Come on up to claim your prize, Joe," the announcer added.

As I walked up to the stage, I noticed another student bring out a black, curly haired puppy. I wasn't sure what kind of dog it was, but it seemed like some sort of toy poodle. The announcer took the dog and handed him to me, saying, "Here is your prize!"

"Wow, a dog," I said, in a mix of excitement and slight apprehension. I didn't know how to take care of a dog. I took him and held him. The puppy was excited and playful, trying to lick my face.

"Any idea what you'd like to call him?" the announcer asked, then put the microphone in front of me.

"I'm not sure yet," I replied.

"Alright! Well think about it and give him a name later tonight. Congratulations, Joe!" she said and everyone applauded again.

When I came back down with the dog, Tom was very excited. He loved dogs and missed his dog that was back home.

"Looks like you have a new housemate!" Tom said excitedly.

"You bet! Wanna hold him?" I asked Tom.

"Yeah," he said and took the dog. I was relieved that Tom liked dogs, hoping he might be able to help take care of the dog too.

"What are you gonna call him?" Tom asked.

"Hmm...how about Joto?"

"Joto? What kind of a name is that?" Tom said mockingly.

"'J' and 'O' for Joe and 'T' and 'O' for Tom," I replied. Tom laughed at me.

"How do you think of such things?" I shrugged. "Alright, Joto it is," he said as he petted the dog.

The rest of the night, all the girls wanted to play with Joto, so I danced around holding my puppy and meeting a bunch of women. When the nuns finally forced everyone to leave, Tom and I walked out with Joto. I couldn't believe I was leaving the dance with a new pet.

On Sunday, it occurred to me that I would have to figure out what to do with Joto while I was in church, class, and the lab – which was most of the day Monday through Friday. Looking down at Joto, who was an untrained puppy,

I had no idea what to do with him. Some of my friends could watch him for short periods, but there still would have been large gaps during the day where he was unattended. Finally, a light bulb went off and I thought: I've got it! I'll hide him in the lab.

The next morning I hurried into the lab before 6:00 am Mass, with Joto in tow. I picked him up and did my best to hide him in the side of my jacket. At that point, he was so small that this worked fairly well. Of course, my caution was unnecessary given that no one was in the lab at this hour. I put Joto in a large storage room that nobody ever seemed to use. After giving him some water and a blanket to rest on, I ran off to church.

I checked on Joto and took him for walks throughout the day. Once classes were done and I was in the lab for hours on end, I could check up on him very easily. After I finished up, I took Joto home and then repeated the same process every weekday. This worked for quite a while, mainly because Father was almost never in the lab. Sister and I would take our lab results up to his office, which was on the second floor.

I'm fairly sure Sister found out about the dog early on and chose to look the other way, saint that she was. I got this notion because she suddenly always avoided the storage room where Joto was. Instead of going in there herself, she'd ask me to fetch any items she needed from that area. As time went by, it seemed that either nobody noticed or nobody cared that I was hiding Joto in the lab for most of the day.

When Thanksgiving rolled around, I figured it would just be Joto and me hanging out on campus for a few days, because I couldn't afford a ticket home. Although I was quite disappointed I couldn't be home for the holiday, I figured at least I had Joto to keep me company. All of my friends were headed to see their respective families.

A few days before break, Tom stopped by to visit me.

"I can't wait to go home," Tom said as he plopped himself down on the couch and put his hands behind his head with a dreamy look on his face. "Mom's turkey, big feast…it will be swell," he said with a jovial grin.

"Should be fun," I replied, then returned to the biology book I was studying.

"When are you leaving for home?"

"I ain't goin' home 'til Christmas," I said without looking up from my book.

"Huh? You have to go home. It's Thanksgiving!" Tom said.

"Can't afford it," I muttered, a bit embarrassed. Tom seemed mildly surprised. I never spoke about my finances, and while our buddies were by no means well off, they must have noticed that I struggled more than they did.

"Oh...that's a shame," Tom replied slowly. "Well, we should try to think of a way to get you home," he added. "You're Italian, Joe! Can't be away from family on a big holiday. I'm gonna think of something..." he started, before getting up and walking around, deep in thought. I chuckled at him and returned to my reading.

A few days later, I heard some loud knocking at the door as I was studying at the kitchen table. Joto had been resting at my feet but ran eagerly to greet our visitor. I got up and answered the door to find Tom and a few of our close friends at the door.

"Is there a party happening here?" I said jokingly as I opened the door for my buddies.

Tom slapped an envelope into my hand, grinning.

"Here you go, Joe!" he announced.

"What's this?" I asked, a bit confused.

"Open it!" my other friend John instructed. I looked at them oddly and opened the envelope to find a train ticket to New Jersey.

"What's this for?"

"We chipped in to help you get a ticket home. Can't stay here all alone for Thanksgiving," Tom said.

"Wow. Gee, thank you, guys," I said, surprised by their generosity. John clapped me on the back.

"Sure thing," Tom said. As soon as the guys left, I hurried upstairs to pack my things. I was humming along, thrilled about how I'd get to see my family so much sooner than I expected when I looked over at Joto and realized that there was no one to watch him over the holiday – so I'd have to sneak him on the train.

CHAPTER 11

Homeward Bound

"Hey, Ma," I practically yelled into the phone.

"Joey!" my mom said exuberantly, sounding shocked to hear her son calling.

"Ma, I'm coming home. Should be home by nighttime."

"My Joey," she crooned. "Annabelle," she yelled off into the distance, "Joey is coming home!" She lowered her voice again and directed it back at me. "Dear Joey, can't wait to see you my boy."

"See you soon, Ma," I replied and was on my way to the station with a small suitcase in hand and Joto in tow. I couldn't wait to see my mom, Annie and Johnny, and the gang. I had a large jacket on so that I could attempt to hide Joto in the side of my coat. He was a fairly quiet dog, but I didn't know how many hours he'd be able to discreetly hide in my coat.

I couldn't think of any other feasible option for Joto while I'd be gone, so I did what I could to wear him out before the train ride. That morning I had taken him for a run until we were both incredibly tired, panting all the way home. After I got my ticket, I approached the platform and waited. I strategically entered one of the cars that didn't have a conductor on it, feeling like a rebel. My heart paced and, despite any efforts to be discreet, I surely drew more attention to myself as I struggled to appear like an average passenger. Joto just sat quietly as I held him propped up with one arm.

A few of the nearby passengers looked questioningly at the large bulge on my side and my awkward stance, but were quickly distracted by their papers or other characters boarding. Once the train was moving, I took a small blanket from my suitcase and put it over Joto and me so that I wouldn't have to worry as much about him peeking out. There wasn't a passenger next to me and after a few hours of reading, I was too tired to stay awake, but kept trying to fight the strong desire to sleep. My eyelids were heavy and would seem to close of their own accord. I'd start in my seat as I woke myself up, finding myself more awake for a brief period. But eventually it was no use and I drifted into a deep slumber.

"Hey, kid!" a man yelled. I startled awake.

"What?" I asked in a harsh tone, almost indignant. What was this guy waking me up for? As I blinked my eyes open, I saw it was one of the train conductors.

"Oh, sir! I'm sorry," I corrected myself. "What is it?" I asked, straightening myself up and remembering Joto was at my side.

"Whatcha got there?" he said in a low voice, looking down toward my side with raised eyebrows. I slowly looked down and saw Joto's tail sticking out beneath the blanket, wagging. I quickly covered his tail with the blanket and looked up at the conductor, my cheeks flushed, unsure what to say. I gazed with wide eyes at his stern countenance. He kept staring at me, looking more and more angry as I waited.

"I...uh..." I sputtered. Looking outside, it was clear I was in the middle of nowhere. There was farmland for miles on end. If he kicked me out at the next stop, I'd have to get another ticket and I didn't have enough money to do that. Suddenly, the conductor laughed. Surprised, I looked at him curiously.

"I'll give you a pass this time...for the holidays. But you can't be bringing a dog on board again, ya hear?" he said in a friendly tone that progressively got more stern.

"Yes, sir," I said. He chuckled a bit and walked off, examining other passengers' tickets. I let out a sigh of relief and peered under the blanket to see Joto looking at me and wagging his tail. I petted him and whispered, "Go to sleep, Joto."

The remainder of the train ride, when the same conductor came through, we averted our eyes. When we made stops with a break, I got out and waited until I was out of sight of the train before letting Joto run around and go to the bathroom. I kept a low profile and once we got to New Jersey, I practically ran off the train in excitement to be home and with relief that I made it there with Joto.

I took a few buses to get home. When I saw the flat, I ran up the steps and exuberantly knocked on the door yelling, "Ma! Annie! Johnny! It's me!" I heard some loud footsteps running toward the door and Johnny opened it.

"Joe! Welcome back, bud," he said as he nearly suffocated me with a massive hug. He stepped back and noticed Joto at his feet. He looked up at me, asking, "Whose dog is that?"

"He's mine – I won him at a dance contest," I explained. "His name is Joto." I picked him up and handed him to Johnny before walking inside. The second I walked in I picked up the scent of marinara sauce wafting from the kitchen. My stomach growled in anticipation of a true Italian meal.

Annie walked out of the kitchen and welcomed me with a warm hug. Then my mom appeared and clung to me as she embraced me, saying, "Joey, my boy."

"Alright, Ma, alright, good to see you too," I said, a bit overwhelmed by her smothering.

"Your dog?" she asked as she stepped back and saw Joto sitting beside me.

"Yeah, didn't I tell you about him?"

"No, son. You never call. Never write," she said wistfully, looking at Annie. I looked at my cousin and saw her shifting her gaze.

"He does write *sometimes*," Annie said, looking at me. I knew what she was referring to – Annie would write letters to my mom that were "from" me in order to make my mom feel better. Annie was always incredibly thoughtful.

"Yeah, Ma. Didn't you get that birthday card I sent you?" I asked, looking at Annie, who nodded in confirmation that she had sent a birthday card from me this year. I smiled at my mom, then at Annie, thankful for her corroboration.

My mom raised her eyebrows. "Nice card," she said a bit sarcastically. Of course she knew it was Annie, not me, who sent her birthday card every year. But she couldn't help being delighted to see me. "Come for dinner. Your favorite: spaghetti."

I took in the smell of the marinara sauce she made, a family recipe passed down from my grandma. It is still one of my favorite scents, always bringing me back to home and my childhood, watching my grandma make an elaborate Italian meal from scratch. When we could afford enough fresh groceries, my grandma would spoil us with incredibly elaborate dinners.

Sitting down to our small, worn wooden table with my mom and cousins, I felt such warmth and joy. St. Louis had become a sort of haven for me, but there's nothing like home.

My trip home was delightful but flew by. My mom was sad to see me leave but thrilled to see Joto go, as his barking kept her up. Back at school, I was saddled with a stack of new research for Father Luyet. One of my assignments involved plotting out data from an experiment. Father didn't tell me how he wanted it done, so I simply plotted out the different points on the graph, then started drawing a line from one point to another. When I brought my graph up to Father's office, he looked at it quizzically and chuckled.

"What's this?" he inquired.

"It's the graph you asked me to make," I replied.

"Why did you draw the line like that? You're supposed to do this," he said as he took his pencil and drew a single line upward diagonally, going through the middle of the scatterplot. Unlike me, he did not particularly connect any of the points to one another. "You're supposed to take an average," he said, lifting his pencil in a pointed manner. This was new to me, so I shrugged.

"Well I didn't get a line like that from the research; I only put the dots where I got my research, so that's why I connected them all," I explained. It was an honest answer. Only someone as naïve as me would have done that, and of course Father chuckled again before he continued to explain how to properly graph the data. Now I laugh at myself, aware that anyone doing this sort of research knew better.

One of my favorite things about Father was his humility. Despite being incredibly intelligent, he took the time to teach me about new things and encouraged me to push forward in times of doubt. I recall that, when I would say something self-deprecating – usually something to the effect of, "Well, I didn't go to an Ivy for undergrad like him" – he would gently remind me that a pedigree didn't define someone.

"You know, Joseph, good students can go to bad schools and bad students can go to good schools," he said. Boy, was he right. Over the years, I came across doctors from all sorts of schools, and always found that the best barometer for a doctor's competency was his or her drive and heart. The alma mater paled in comparison. The best doctors I knew were the ones who cared most about their patients. Simple as that.

I kept up my routine with Joto and felt I had it down to a T. On one typical day I arrived early at the lab, put Joto in his hiding spot, and got to work. Sister Mary mentioned that Father had an important visitor coming by later. This was Sister's gentle way of saying, "Make sure you're on your very best behavior, Joseph."

Father Luyet often had visitors, typically scientists he worked with or potential new professors for the school. One Friday afternoon I had been particularly busy between experiments and other coursework. I was scrambling trying to get everything squared away and realized I hadn't checked on Joto for a while. I rushed over to the supply room and opened the door to find Joto bolting out. "Joto, come back here!" I said in a frustrated, hushed tone.

Attempting to discreetly chase after Joto, I looked around, thankfully finding the lab empty. Joto was fast and playful at times and on this particular day he had an unusual amount of energy. I kept searching for him in vain. I was telling myself I really needed to train him better when I heard footsteps coming down the stairs. My heartbeat quickened as I thought *I hope that isn't Father.*

"And here is the main lab," Father's distinct voice announced. *Oh no*, I said to myself. I looked each way in search of Joto but instead found a pile of his droppings. I suppressed a desire to curse and weighed my options: Father would be down here in thirty seconds. I could either rush to try and clean it up or go after Joto. I decided to search for Joto, figuring I could hide his waste easier than I could hide a dog running out in the open.

Father continued talking to his guest as I ran around in search of my dog as quietly as I could. Finally I saw his curly black hair protruding from a space beneath the bottom of a shelf. *Gotcha!* I thought. I scooped him up and scurried over to the storage room where I kept him, quickly placing him in and gently shutting the door with a soft click. Father was approaching the lab, so I rushed over to where Joto did his business and stood in front of it, attempting to block Father and his guest from seeing it. I actually hoped they would simply pass through on the other side of the lab without saying a word to me. Unfortunately, Father caught my eye and veered toward me in a friendly manner.

"Ahh, Joseph," he said gently, "meet Professor Zweig. He's visiting from Yale."

"How do you do?" Professor Zweig said as he held out his hand. I stood awkwardly, still trying to shield any view of Joto's excrement. I shook his hand.

"Nice to meet you, Sir," I said, while stealing a glance at Father and seeing him wrinkle his nose in disgust. He looked around a bit and then down at my feet, and of course noticed what Joto had done.

He shot me a reprimanding look. "Dog's gotta go, Joseph," he said, raising his eyebrows and appearing embarrassed. My cheeks reddened.

"Yes, Father. Sorry. I'll clean this up right away," I said as I went off to clean and take Joto home. I realized that Father had probably known about the dog too, but figured it wasn't a problem if he was never in the way.

"I apologize…" I heard Father begin to say to his guest, before he went on and discussed more about his studies in cryobiology. Fortunately, the esteemed professor laughed it off and was far more interested in freezing experiments than my dog's antics.

On my walk home, Joto trotted happily at my side and I wondered what I would do with him. I looked down at him wagging his tail and picking up a scent, completely unaware that I couldn't keep him anymore.

After some searching around the campus, I ended up asking one of the lunch ladies, Jeanine, if she knew of anyone who might want a dog. Jeanine was a cheerful, large black woman who was always talkative.

"What kind of dog?" she asked me, appearing somewhat interested.

"I think he's a poodle. Real small with black, curly hair. He's well behaved and friendly. Pretty smart, too," I began, thinking of what else to say to her.

"Hmmm," she said thoughtfully. "Bring him by. My kids really want a dog. If he's as good as you say, I might just take him." Relieved, I ran home to get Joto.

I brought him right back and Jeanine's face lit up when she saw the little guy. I picked him up and handed him to her. She cradled him and looked down at him lovingly.

"How cute!" she exclaimed. "My kids would love him."

"Well why don't you take him home and see how it goes? If you don't want him, I'll find someone else who does." She agreed and ended up loving Joto. I was delighted that I found him a good home, because I really wasn't prepared to care for a dog. Although I missed Joto, I knew he'd be much better off at a house with a yard and a family to give him plenty of attention.

Toward the end of my second year, I applied to several medical schools, figuring I would go to whichever one accepted me first. I've always liked to go with the path of least resistance. The day I found an envelope addressed to me from the Kirksville College of Osteopathic Medicine, my heart started pounding. I took a breath and ripped open the envelope, letting it fall to the floor as I quickly read my acceptance letter. I was ecstatic to know I was accepted and would attend Kirksville, which was in a more rural part of Missouri. I had studied for so many years, dreaming of becoming a doctor, and now it felt as if nothing was in my way. The only downside to my new plan was that I'd have to break the news to Father and Sister.

Many weeks went by and I figured I didn't need to tell my mentors about pursuing medical school quite yet. However, one day while I was working with Sister, Father started talking about how he wanted me to pursue a Ph.D in biophysics and I realized I couldn't put off telling them much longer. I was touched and proud that he wanted me to continue studying under him, but had to confess that I was changing schools to pursue medicine. I explained that I had wanted to stay at St. Louis, but was not accepted to its medical school. After I delivered the news, he looked down with a long face for a second before returning to his typical countenance.

"Was this your plan all along?" he asked me gently. He seemed curious, but not at all upset.

I nodded. "It was my plan all along," I said simply. "I've wanted to be a doctor for a long time." I looked over at Sister, who seemed more disappointed.

"Congratulations on your acceptance," she said graciously.

"Thank you, Sister Mary."

A few weeks later, after a Saturday morning Mass, Sister Mary caught up to me as I was sleepily trudging back to my house.

"What has you down, Joseph?" she asked sincerely.

"What do you mean?" I replied, playing dumb.

"You have a heavy heart today. What's wrong?"

"Well…" I began, wondering if I should tell her why I was stressed. "I need a microscope for medical school. But I can't afford one." I felt ashamed and wondered how I would get the money to pay for the equipment. I certainly wasn't going to ask my mother. Sister looked at me and nodded. There was silence for a few moments.

"Will you come into the lab with me briefly, Joseph? I want to show you something," she said, changing the subject. Although I was unsure of why she would want me to come in on a Saturday morning, I immediately agreed. I revered Sister and would do nearly whatever she asked me to do.

Once we were in the lab, Sister invited me to have a seat at the table. "I'll be right back," she said. I sat down, wondering what was going on. I wasn't supposed to be working and Sister never had me come to the lab without an assignment. As I waited, I looked at the freezing apparatus I had helped build earlier in the year. I sighed, knowing I would miss this place, especially Father and Sister.

A few minutes went by before I heard Sister's footsteps. I turned around and saw her slowly walking, cradling a large microscope. She approached me and delicately set it down with a small smile. "This is for you," she said.

My jaw must have dropped; I was so stunned. I stared down at the pristine microscope in awe. I looked back up at Sister, then back down at the microscope, unsure what to say.

"Sister...thank you," I finally managed to mutter.

"You're welcome, Joseph. We will certainly miss you around here. I am so proud of you – you will be a wonderful doctor." After saying my goodbyes, I walked home carefully carrying my microscope, thinking about how Sister never ceased to amaze me.

I never forgot Sister's generosity. I also never forgot the microscope she gave me. I've brought it with me everywhere I've moved since then. When I moved into my current home, I actually placed it on a desk across from the entryway. It's still there to this day.

CHAPTER 12

A True Romantic

MEDICAL SCHOOL WAS BUSY FROM the second I arrived. I wound up at Kirksville College of Osteopathic Medicine (which is now A.T. Still University). Becoming a doctor of osteopathy (DO) was not my first choice – I would have preferred an MD, but a DO was still a doctor and I wanted to continue on that path.

Kirksville was the mother of all DO schools, because it was the world's first osteopathic medicine school. I found the history of DOs quite interesting. DOs became quite successful in the early 1900s because of the epidemic flu in that era. People died like flies. And MDs were very unsuccessful. In fact, many people were more likely to die from MD treatments because the medications they gave at that time were not standardized by pharmaceutical companies (which were in their infancy). The products were often toxic, impure, and inconsistent. As a result, many people being medicated at that time were worse off after treatment.

However, if people went to a DO, they weren't given dangerous medications. Instead, the DO would manipulate and massage the patients' muscles, which mobilized the lymphatic system through the musculoskeletal system. This type of adjustment allowed the patient's body to recover on its own. And eventually that's what happens. The body makes its own medicine, actually. Sometimes all you have to do is get the "medications" the body makes to the proper areas of the person's body.

Medical school was busy from the start and I found myself studying day and night. I ended up joining a fraternity, Theta Psi, which was my first time experiencing Greek life (Farleigh Dickinson did not have any fraternities).

The Theta Psi guys were known as the gentlemen. There was also the Atlas Club, which had the reputation of being the ruffians. There was also a Jewish frat, which probably had the most polite men.

I always figured my fraternity was a cut above the Atlas Club. We were a little more polished. That doesn't mean we were any morally better or any-thing…it was mostly a bunch of rich, rather spoiled guys, other than me.

There wasn't much time for parties, despite the presence of fraternities. However, every year there was one party that stopped the whole town: Sadie Hawkins Day. Literally everything closed on Sadie Hawkins Day, to the extent that – legend had it – some surgeons may have even been pulled out of surgery. After a couple of years, the town actually banned the festivities because things got so rowdy.

Apart from the sparse social gatherings, most of my time was spent with my books. The first six months were a test – if we didn't make good marks, we would be thrown out. In fact, the president of our class got thrown out at the six month mark because he didn't make the cut. That was a sobering piece of news to many of us and a wake up call about the importance of our grades.

Studying in my $20 per month room, 1956

At one point, I got a notice that the school wasn't going to release my grades because I had missed a payment. I didn't have time to work in med school and money was tight. I didn't know what to do. I called home and told my mom about it but didn't ask her for any money, because she didn't have any either. I started thinking about where I might be able to get a quick job. Asking people for money made me uncomfortable and I truly didn't have much free time to do anything other than my schoolwork.

Yet the next week I got an envelope in the mail with enough cash to make my payment and receive my grades again. It was accompanied by a letter from Lou, saying that he and Horace asked around the neighborhood and got a bunch of people to chip in to help me out. That was the kind of place I grew up in. Nobody had much money, but we were there for each other. Even though they were street kids, my childhood buddies wanted to see me succeed and that gave me a great deal of confidence in myself and in the quality of our friendship.

Although my grades were good, I had so much respect for medicine that no matter how high my marks were, I always knew there was a vast amount more I needed to understand before I could become a bona fide doctor. As a result, I over-studied a lot of the time, which as it turns out, is a strategy students can use to do well in school.

Before arriving at Kirksville, I had never lived in such a small town. There were a few shops and such, but it was mostly an area surrounded by farmland. The expansiveness of it all made me miss home sometimes. I thought about Dolores, who I still dated every time I visited home. We wrote each other love letters and though I met other lovely women at medical school, I missed the comfort of being with Dolores.

My buddies must have caught on to my romantic tendencies, because they would tease me a bit about how quickly I fell for girls. Once, before one of our labs started, we were talking about love and all that and romance came up. And my classmate Tom said, "You know what? Joe is the only romantic guy among us. All of us just see the trees and the water, but Joe sees the trees, the water, and the sky." The others nodded their heads in concurrence.

As time went by, it seemed more and more likely, at least to other people, that Dolores and I would marry. My mother adored her, which was important to me. While I was away at medical school, she would visit my mom and help her out around the house. My mom told me she even scrubbed her floors. Dolores would have made a great wife, given her nurturing qualities – she was all about family.

Eventually my mom and Dolores came to visit me at Kirksville. At this point, it finally became clear to me that she wanted to marry me. I was young and not ready for that kind of commitment, but didn't realize that at the time. Although I was thrilled to see Dolores at first, things changed after we spent some more time together.

On a hot summer day, we made plans to meet at the pool. She arrived before me and was already in the water when I sat up on the deck to soak up some heat before jumping in. I asked her to join me at the lounge chairs and watched her as she got out of the pool.

As she got out of the water, I admired her – she had a beautiful face and great hair and as far as I was concerned, had a perfect body. I had never seen her in so little before. Yet toward the end of that trip, I felt that Dolores wasn't the girl I wanted to marry. Or maybe I simply felt I wasn't ready to be married to anyone.

Sometimes it's hard to believe, even now, that my feelings for a girl I loved so much changed so instantaneously. Of course, I didn't say anything to Dolores, but when she returned home, I stopped writing letters and eventually, she got the message. On my next visit home, I found out she had a new boyfriend. This didn't come as a surprise. After all, I had stopped talking to her. Many doctors at the hospital she worked at wanted to marry her, so she continued on her path toward marriage and I continued mine toward becoming a doctor with the perfect woman at my side. The first step was becoming a doctor and in med school, most of my attention and devotion went to science. I figured I would find the right woman at the right time.

CHAPTER 13

I Am The Doctor

———

MY CLASSMATE MENDEN AND I drove along a dirt road, creating a trail of dust behind us, approaching the small shantytown where we served as doctors. The town was called Hurdland and as a part of our medical school education, students were paired off to serve small, impoverished areas in the middle of nowhere.

Being a doctor in the boonies was interesting for a few reasons: It was my first time practicing as a "doctor," I technically wasn't a doctor yet, and I had never interacted with people in such a rural, dilapidated town. Most of the homes in Hurdland didn't have running water or electricity.

One of my first patients in Hurdland was a little boy who was running a high fever. Menden watched as I checked his temperature. We exchanged looks of concern when we saw the thermometer read 102 degrees. The boy had all sorts of splotches on his skin and the whites of his eyes had a reddish tint.

I took my classmate aside and said, "Menden, this boy is really sick. He needs a doctor." Menden raised his eyebrows in a comedic manner. I realized what I had said and corrected myself: "I am the doctor."

"That's right. We're the doctors," Menden said with a small laugh. I looked at him in concern.

"Oh, boy. What have we gotten ourselves into, Menden?" I said jokingly.

"Looks like measles, wouldn't you say?"

"Yeah. We've got to get him in some sort of isolation so he doesn't start spreading it around."

The most memorable case in Hurdland occurred one of the few times we went out at night. It was late and pitch black as we drove in and, just like every other time we drove out, I thought about how we would be screwed if we had any car problems. Venturing out of civilization and into this shantytown was far more worrisome at night; the road ahead was only illuminated by the stars, moon, and our headlights. No one was around for many miles.

When we pulled in, we had no idea what we would have in store, as usual. A kid came running out to us and yelled, "Doctors! Hurry!" We grabbed our bags, running after him, following his lead into one of the shacks. The kid held up a flashlight, revealing a woman sitting there with another woman standing above her, holding a towel to her head. The towel was all red, soaked in blood. Both women were in tears. The boy cringed as he looked at the woman, who might have been his mother. He tried to hold the flashlight steady, but his hand was trembling.

Though I wondered what had happened, there was no time to waste. I put on my gloves in a hurry, then rushed over to help. The woman holding the towel knowingly moved. My patient was very pale and weak from the rapid blood loss. I peeled the towel back slowly and saw a huge laceration in the woman's head. It would certainly need to be stitched up.

"I'll hold the light," Menden said to the boy. He gladly handed it over to Menden and retreated back into a corner. Now the stream of light was steady and I could get to work. Menden and I didn't need to communicate much about who would do what during an emergency. We each had our areas of specialty. One of mine was suturing. After my experience at Passaic General, where I was allowed to suture patients as a scrub nurse, I was pretty good at stitching up wounds. However, I didn't have the proper materials to do a traditional suture; our service in the boonies was usually for standard ailments and illnesses, not injured patients requiring surgery.

My only choice was to sew her up with what we had: a needle and thread. As I worked my way through her injury, with nothing but Menden's flashlight and a basic needle and thread, I was incredibly thankful that the doctors in Passaic used to let me sew up. Fortunately, I picked it up quickly back then and by now, I looked and felt like a natural.

Once I finished, Menden and I let out a sigh of relief. The poor woman had undergone the stitching with nothing to numb her pain. She thanked us when we finished, though she was in a state of shock and immense pain. I wished we could have done more to help, but as we were walking out the door, we were immediately solicited by others with sick family members. As weeks went by, we were able to confirm that the woman healed well. Menden and I were relieved to know that the patient's suffering wasn't in vain.

Part II

———

CHAPTER 14

Hollywood Bound

THE FOUR YEARS AT KIRKSVILLE went by fairly quickly, given the demanding workload. Before graduation, I started applying for my internship. All doctors had to do a one-year rotating internship before they could begin their residency. Many of my classmates were looking for internships in their hometowns or at least somewhere in the Midwest. Some of the ones who were more concerned about reputation were seeking work in New York City. But me, I only wanted to be one place: Los Angeles.

After graduation, 1959

I had never been out West and the glamour of Hollywood had always been alluring to me. Although I would be working in medicine, not in movies, I would still be close to that scene and perhaps even meet some movie stars and directors, I figured. It also seemed so exotic. I had never been to the West Coast and I thought of it as a sort of tropical place.

As graduation approached, my mom called and asked how she would get to the ceremony. The trip from Newark to St. Louis was a full day and I wondered how, in fact, she would be able to find her way, given that she never traveled anywhere outside of the neighboring towns of Garfield. I thought about how confused she'd be and how difficult it would be for her to ask for directions, considering her broken English and illiteracy. Then an idea popped in my mind: Menden's mother lived near Garfield and I wondered if she might be able to meet my mom and show her the way.

Menden's mom, Susan, said she'd be happy to help out so we arranged for my mom to meet her at the Newark train station. So here was my Sicilian mother with her broken English traveling with Menden's mom, who certainly knew how to read and write well – she was Jewish. By the time Menden and I met them at the train station in St. Louis, my mom and Mrs. Schwartz seemed to be old friends, laughing and smiling to each other.

On our ride back, Menden and I threw them a quizzical look when my mom called Mrs. Schwartz "Pillowcase."

"Pillowcase? What are you talking about?" I laughed, wondering how my mom could have possibly mixed up the name "Susan" with "pillowcase." Mrs. Schwartz proceeded to explain that when they were on the train, they noticed a young girl with a baby who seemed absolutely beside herself. They offered to help her out and she gave them a look of appreciation and took them up on the offer.

For hours on the train, my mom and Mrs. Schwartz took turns caring after the baby so that the young woman could get some much needed rest. They also helped her figure out what to do with the baby's diapers, because there was no place to throw them out on the train. Finding no other viable option, my mom glanced at one of the pillows, pulled off the pillowcase, and started storing the soiled diapers there. The young mother was pleased to find a makeshift trash bag and my mom and Mrs. Schwartz found the situation funny enough to start nicknaming each other "pillowcase."

Although our mothers just shared those short train rides together, they built a bond and would call each other every so often, always beginning the conversation with, "Hello, Pillowcase!" It always warms my heart to think of how these two women from such different worlds met to go see their sons graduate and quickly became friends.

Our actual graduation was a traditional ceremony. After I got my diploma and the ceremony was over, I found my mother and she looked at me with such pride in her eyes. She grabbed my hands and squeezed them, saying, "My Joey" with a big smile. My mom never once told me, "I'm proud of you," but she didn't need to. Just as we never really said, "I love you" or "thank you," her pride was a sentiment that was strongly felt; we didn't actually need to say the words to sense the other person's pride, love, or gratitude. Our actions demonstrated our affection and appreciation.

After graduation, I stayed on for about a week to participate in a workshop on EKG reading. I didn't know much about it, but cardiovascular health was a particular point of interest of mine and I always tried to get my hands on any new medical knowledge I could. With my certification in EKG readings completed, I traveled back home to 45 Harrison Ave. For the first time in my life, I flew on an airplane.

I knew I wouldn't be home long, because I'd find out where I was accepted to intern soon, but I wanted to get some work experience in.

It was a small town and word got around that I was back. It was delightful to see my old buddies. Most of them stayed local and would spend the rest of their lives in Garfield or a nearby town.

After graduating medical school, I thought I knew a vast amount about being a doctor. But I was quickly learning that there was a great deal I didn't know. I would soon get the chance to discover a lot more, though, as I got my acceptance to intern in Los Angeles. With the letter in hand, sitting in my childhood flat in Garfield, I started dreaming of the new life I was creating for myself – the prestige of being a doctor, the adventure of going out west, and the money I would earn. Finally, I'd be able to give my mom a better life. And I'd be able to experience the place I had dreamed of since I was a child, working as an usher. I was off to Hollywood.

CHAPTER 15

Landing In Los Angeles

––––––––

THE ONLY THING STANDING BETWEEN me and Hollywood was a cross-country flight. As I waited to board, I began to feel my nerves ramp up. It was bad enough to go on any flight, but this would be by far the longest flight I had ever been on. Fortunately, they served drinks on the plane and that helped ease the flight anxiety. When we were beginning our descent, I looked out the window at the vast, sprawling city below me. Even from the plane, I could feel the warmth of it and could sense the dryness of the mountains after the summer months.

As I got off the plane in LA, I remember thinking, "Where are the coconuts?" On the ride over to the hospital, I was also looking at the tall palm trees, wondering why they didn't have any of the tropical fruit. I went straight from LAX to Doctor's Hospital[1], where I was welcomed and given a tour. It was hard to believe that my years of work were finally coming together – I would be interning for a brief time, then I would become a resident and officially be a doctor.

Other than summer jobs, I made no money in medical school, so I was thrilled to be getting a paycheck. As an intern, we were paid $65 a month, plus free room and board. This kind of money was something I had never seen in my life. I felt rich. So I went out and bought a nice car.

I came whizzing through the hospital parking lot in a black convertible the next day, turning heads as I drove by with a wide smile across my face.

––––––––

1 Doctor's Hopsital was on Jefferson St. at the time, but no longer exists.

Later that day, some of the other interns nicknamed me "The King." I felt like a big shot. I was in Los Angeles for my internship with a cool car and the attention of any student nurse I wanted.

I shared a room in a building across from the hospital with three other interns. One of the others was also Italian, one was Jewish, and the other was a redneck. Of the four of us, I was the only one who could read EKGs. It turned out staying for that free optional workshop to learn how to read EKGs at St. Louis was a great idea. I had no idea how well it would serve me later on; I simply went out of interest, to learn more about medicine.

Although it wasn't surprising that the other interns didn't know how to read EKGs, I was a bit shocked when, a few weeks into my internship, I learned I was the only one in the entire hospital who could read them. Doctor's Hospital was a small hospital and EKGs weren't mainstream yet, but their prevalence would grow at an exponential rate. Although I didn't know it at the time, the decision to take the class to read EKGs was a pivotal career decision. It automatically positioned me with a specialized skill that would become indispensible in the fight against the top killer in the country: heart disease.

Starting the internship, I didn't know what to expect. I knew it was a rotating internship, which meant I'd be in different areas of medicine to learn the basics and prove my medical ability. The one portion of the internship that I hated was that I had to deliver 125 babies. The actual delivery was fine; I didn't mind that. What made this task an annoyance was the amount of waiting around necessary before the babies were born.

Given that I worked long hours, I often got tired during the time period of waiting for a baby to be delivered. The duration of labor was always unpredictable, of course, so I also never knew how long I'd be waiting. Although the mother-to-be was in pain and stressed out, she had nurses caring for her; my role was solely to deliver the baby. So while I waited, my eyes would often drift and I'd fall asleep. Naturally, if the patient noticed that her doctor was asleep as she was going through her labor pains, she'd often get pretty pissed.

There were many times I woke to a patient, or sometimes a nurse, screaming at me. Something to the effect of, "What are you doing?" or "You can't fall asleep!" I'd start as they were yelling and I would hastily apologize. Once they calmed back down, I'd try my best not to fall asleep again, but sometimes I did.

Naturally, once the delivery was in progress, I was always alert and ready to tackle possible complications. Most of these deliveries happened without incident or if there was a complication, I was instructed to call in a more senior doctor.

There was only one occasion where the wait time for a senior doctor was frighteningly long. Back in the late fifties, it was common to do an episiotomy, which is a surgical cut made at the vaginal opening in order to make more room for the baby to be born. One patient was clearly having a difficult time delivering and it was clear from my training that I should do an episiotomy. But once I delivered the baby, the open wound was gushing with blood – far more than what was within the range of normal bleeding.

Before I did anything, I told the nearest nurse to run and get one of the senior doctors. There wasn't any time to waste, so I quickly began suturing the wound, finally getting the bleeding to abate. The doctor I called for came in just as I was finishing up and I explained what had happened. He observed my work and said something like, "Looks like it's under control now. Good work, Joe." The poor mother was drained of energy and had lost a lot of blood, but I knew she would be fine now that the bleeding was stopped. Once the doctor had approved of my work, I could breathe easy again.

While work was my main priority and took up the vast majority of my time, I didn't take my free time for granted – instead I spent it exploring the nearby parts of Los Angeles and soaking in the warmth and glamour of it all. And, of course, dating women. The first time I drove around Beverly Hills and along the Sunset Strip, it was simply added confirmation that I came to the right place. In time, the Sunset Strip would become my favorite place to go out and meet women. In those early days, though, I had my hands full dating a ton of student nurses and their friends.

Toward the end of my internship, I started dating a beautiful girl named Barbara, who I quickly fell for. She was of Swedish descent and had it all – charm, beauty, wit. To say she was a knockout was an understatement. Barbara lived in Long Beach, where we'd spend the weekends together. Those weekends were paradise – out on the beach or even a boat with a gorgeous blond by my side. Not much time went by before she introduced me to her parents. When she pulled up to a beach house, I felt a bit intimidated, but also curious and impressed. There was even a boat anchored in front, which was also theirs. I stood there, in their gorgeous home, looking out the large glass panel windows to the glimmering ocean with their yacht gently swaying with the current. Then there was little me, with a nickel.

But Barbara believed in me and I had a promising career ahead as I was nearing the end of my internship. Unlike most women, Barbara would often call me out on my antics. I used to tell her, "I got culture" after I'd say something intellectual. Anytime I said that, she'd start imitating me, saying, "I got cult-cha, I got cult-cha" and I'd crack up at her impression of my accent.

We were from different worlds and had very different ambitions. I spent most of my days in the hospital while Barbara won beauty pageants. Walking into a restaurant with her on my arm turned heads, often accompanied by envious glances. I was proud to call her my girlfriend and she was madly in love with me.

At that age I was truly naïve about what women wanted and what they expected. When Barbara suggested we put a deposit in for a ring, I complied, not thinking much of it. In fact, I think I forgot about it after a few weeks. On the occasional weekend that we stayed at her parents', they would naturally have us stay in different rooms. Barbara would sneak in my room in the middle of the night and I would get nervous and say, "What are you doing? We're at your parents'!" She found my concern and "old fashioned" mindset endearing.

Barbara and I often spent time with our respective friends, doing anything from spending time on the beach, going to restaurants, or even playing sports. When some of my buddies organized a coed touch football game, I was eager to bring Barbara along and show her how to play the sport that was such a huge part of my childhood.

The game was going well and although Barbara didn't know how to properly throw a football, she could run fast and the game wasn't competitive anyway, so it didn't really matter. By this time, I was incredibly in love with her and admired everything about her – the way the sun hit her blond hair, her one hundred watt smile, sparkling eyes, perfect body, and her sense of humor. Someone could have easily run in to me and knocked me over as I was distracted watching her try to play football.

Finally she caught the football and started running the other way. Everyone was surprised to see her making a good play and she humorously put the football under her shirt as she ran, as if hiding it. And without any warning, I had this image of her being overweight and pregnant in my head. Just like I had with another girl I loved, in a moment, something switched in my brain and I never felt as in love with Barbara again.

We kept dating for a while and things were fun and fine – I still loved her, but there was now doubt in my mind. Barbara must have sensed this, as she seemed to pull away a bit. Plus, her life was taking her to new heights. She entered the Miss California pageant and I was swelling with pride when I walked around telling people I was dating someone in the running to be Miss California. And then she won the title. Naturally, I was even more proud to announce my girlfriend was Miss California. But after a while, the title went to her head.

Eventually she cut things off with me, which was a huge disappointment. I was never sure why she ended things. In hindsight, it may have been that I never followed through with proposing. I put the deposit on the ring but never actually went to buy it in full and put it on her finger. Her absence was felt strongly for a while, but there were of course many other women out there. I started dating again and though I never forgot her, I didn't regret my lack of a proposal. I was too young to get married and after all, my love for her didn't feel as true as I always imagined it should; it certainly didn't feel comparable to the sweeping romances I watched at the cinema in my youth.

There were two people at Doctor's Hospital who became my mentors. They were smart Jewish doctors who kindly took me under their wing after I expressed an unusual amount of interest in their work. I always tried to learn as much as I could and from my experiences as a scrub nurse and working with Dr. Luyet in graduate school, I knew the best way to learn was to work side-by-side with experts. So whenever I could, I followed the two doctors around, soaking in as much knowledge as possible.

After all the deliveries and the year-long internship were complete, I finally got my DO degree and my license to practice. One hundred and twenty-five deliveries in a single year was a lot, especially considering that was just one aspect of the internship. When I completed those deliveries, I was pleased to know I wouldn't have to continue with that kind of work, which required so much waiting.

At twenty-nine years old, I realized my childhood dream and became a doctor. Now that I was accustomed to the Los Angeles lifestyle, I certainly didn't want to go anywhere else. Fortunately, I was able to secure my residency at Los Angeles County General Hospital, which was quite competitive. You couldn't just get into County – you had to have pull. The Jewish doctors who mentored me during my internship knew people at County and helped me get in. Of course, you also had to pass the Civil Service Exam, which I did on all accounts.

Once I had my acceptance to County secured, I came across another opportunity. Another intern spoke about how he was going to Detroit and some of us gave him an apologetic look, thinking he was unable to get into a more desirable location. Yet he quickly corrected us and explained that it was his first choice – he was going to a private hospital that had a lot of money, where his salary would be far superior over the long run. His explanation and the promise of this seemingly rich hospital piqued my interest and after some further investigation, I also applied for the same residency in Detroit. Another reason I was interested in it was that it was an Osteopathic hospital, which was the type of medicine I studied in medical school.

When I got in and accepted the position at Detroit Osteopathic Hospital, my mentors were surprised. I believe one of them said, "You turned down County? No one turns down County." But I was resolute in my plan and thought I was off to a place where my salary would be significantly higher. For a kid who grew up with so little, the idea of making more money by simply being in a less desirable location was too tempting to pass up.

Although I was antsy to start my residency, I had a few months off before it began, so I returned home to spend time with family and friends. I was only home a few days before I was itching to begin medical work again, so I started looking for jobs I may be able to work for the summer. I ended up asking Dr. Catania, the local family doctor who first inspired my own career aspirations, if he needed any assistance and he suggested I come along and do some work for him.

For the next few months, I followed Dr. Catania around town and helped him with more minor cases, like treating babies with a fever. Between my hands-on experience in the rural clinics in med school and my year at Doctor's Hospital, I thought I knew everything I needed to know. But I quickly realized that, like other new doctors, I didn't know what the hell I was doing. We all thought we knew what we were doing, but in many instances, we didn't know shit. It takes a great deal of time and practice before a doctor has any place to tout his ability.

Dr. Catania's modesty was one of his most admirable traits. While I sought out a prestigious, alluring place to work, my family doctor worked all his life in our Italian neighborhood and a few others nearby. He became a part of the fabric of the community and was everyone's doctor. Back when I was growing up, at least in our neighborhood, no one was really seeing specialists. So if you had an ailment, you called Catania.

Out in California, the relationships people had with their doctors were quite different – generally far less personal. It was simply a different culture. It was also a different time period and medicine was getting more specialized. Despite the different approaches, I knew I wanted to incorporate the sense of caring and generosity I'd received as a child into my own practice. Working under Dr. Catania was a poignant reminder of the doctor-patient relationship I'd grown up with, which was wonderful to experience before I officially started my residency. Although I didn't know what the culture would be like in Detroit, I wanted to emulate Dr. Catania's work ethic and generosity wherever I practiced.

CHAPTER 16

The Doctor Is In (Residency)

———

ARRIVING FOR RESIDENCY WAS A new milestone and that sense of accomplishment was present as I strutted into Detroit Osteopathic Hospital for my first day. But that enthusiasm was short-lived. It only took a few days of experiencing my residency in Detroit to realize I had made a huge mistake. After a long day, I sat down and realized I had given up perfect weather and all the excitement of being near Hollywood for a job that was far more difficult and, as it turned out, paid only marginally more.

Work at Detroit was far more demanding because of the culture of the hospital. Because it was a private institution, they didn't want to give interns much responsibility, which was smart; there was less risk having residents do virtually all of the work. After all, the residents had already been interns. This was only problematic for the residents, who were now doing intern work in addition to all their normal responsibilities.

I called friends who had gone on to Los Angeles County General Hospital (which we simply called "County") to compare notes and was only driven more into my sense of regret when they shared their experience. They told me that at County, interns were given a great deal of responsibility, which lightened the residents' workload. One of my friends who had interned at Doctor's Hospital told me about how much harder the interns at County had to work and remarked I should be glad we interned at Doctor's Hospital. And I was glad about that, but I was more preoccupied with regret about my return to the Midwest.

Of course, Detroit wasn't all bad. The nurses there were beautiful, kind Midwestern girls and I had a lot of them hustling me. That helped combat the cold weather and dearth of social activity (compared to Los Angeles). For the most part, I was simply focused on my residency and learning as much as I could. Living at the hospital made it easy to avoid the cold weather in the middle of winter. Some days I would walk from my room to work and then back without ever going outside.

About halfway through, I called up one of my buddies at Doctor's Hospital, exasperated with my choice and homesick for California.

"I've made a huge mistake!" I lamented to my friend. "I've got to find a way back to County." There was silence on the other end. We both knew how hard it was to get in to County in the first place; there was no way they were going to take back someone who rejected them. Nevertheless, I would try. I wasn't ever one to accept the status quo or what other people claimed was "just the way it is." If I were that type of person, I never would have made it to medical school.

My next calls were to my mentors at Doctor's Hospital, the two Jewish doctors who initially helped me get into County. They were pleased to hear from me but their responses weren't encouraging.

"Joe, I don't think they really take people back," one of them said, "but we'll try our best."

I figured it couldn't hurt to reapply. As I put my application in the mail, I sighed and figured that whatever happened, I tried my best. I knew that being in Detroit would be fine, but it felt as if I'd left a part of myself in Hollywood.

As luck would have it, they gave me a chance to return to County. After receiving that letter, I went out to celebrate. Most of my friends there had lived in a small Midwestern town their whole lives and didn't quite understand my jubilance about getting out of town, but politely congratulated me nonetheless.

When I pulled up to County a few months later, I let out a sigh of relief. It felt like I had won a battle, fighting my way back to Los Angeles. I took in the sunshine for a few moments before triumphantly walking back into the hospital.

Being a resident in Los Angeles was a whole new ballgame. As an intern, I had far less responsibility because there were residents supervising me. Now, as a resident, I had five interns under me and each of those interns had a medical student shadowing them; often times there was a parade following me wherever I went.

At Doctor's Hospital, being an intern was certainly demanding, but I quickly saw how much harder it was to be an intern at County. My friend who told me to count my blessings about my own intern days was right – County's interns were far more overworked than we were at Doctor's Hospital. Just like things had differed from Doctor's Hospital and Detroit Osteopathic Hospital, the culture was different at County as well. For whatever reason, they assigned far more work to the interns; the interns did virtually all the scut work for the doctors. That's not to say the residents had it easy. Everyone was working incredibly hard. But being a resident at County was far more manageable than it had been in Detroit.

At County, I had another opportunity to live at the hospital at a great rate: twenty dollars per month for food and room and board. I'd have one roommate and our room would be in a building just across from the hospital. I didn't consider any other option and signed up to live at County.

When I was settling into my room I wondered who my roommate would be and hoped he'd be a fun guy to spend time with, as we'd see each other nearly all day between our residency and rooming situation. As I was unpacking, I heard the lock turning and looked up to see who was coming in. And there was a tall, suave guy who smiled at me and introduced himself as Vic. Between the way he carried himself and his smart outfit, you knew Vic came from a well-heeled family.

Vic and I were from opposite worlds. Whereas I was raised by a poor immigrant on the East Coast, he grew up in Malibu with wealthy parents, who were doctors. Not only were they doctors, his father was actually the Associate Dean of a nearby medical school and his mom was a respected Ph.D. who taught at the med school too.

I learned a lot from Vic. He was polished, daring, intelligent, and hard-working. Although he came from money and could have probably skated by doing far less, he became a doctor. Instead of acting like a spoiled brat, he always came off as refined and gentlemanly – like he was the George Hamilton of the medical world. Always cool and collected, twenty steps ahead of everyone else.

I instantly admired Vic, if only because of his class. I never had class like him. I had the looks, but no class. That's all I had going for me: my looks and my job as a doctor. And for many girls, that was enough. Sometimes Vic would get frustrated with me because I'd steal his girlfriends. He mostly found this funny, because it was so easy for him to find another girl. There were certainly a few times he got upset, but he was so calm and collected that he'd barely show it. At least later on in life, once we were both married, he thought it was hilarious.

But back then, with all these girls and a shared room, I'd have to find hours where Vic was away so that I could have some time alone with them. And once it was just us, I had my routine. I'd offer the girl a drink, then I'd run down to the next level to the ice machine, then run back up to mix the drink.

Fortunately, Vic liked to go out a lot. I found a lot of student nurses hustling me as a resident at County too. The one who is most memorable was Jen, who looked like a model and talked like a lady out of a classic film. She was crazy about me and though I was infatuated with her, it never developed into a deeper love. We had some great times together, though. In one instance we were making love and broke the bed, causing us to roll off onto the floor. Once we realized it wasn't an earthquake (just our own exuberance) we erupted in a fit of laughter. When Vic walked in late that night and found me trying to fix the bed, he looked at me with a raised brow and a sly grin. I explained why the bed was broken and gave him a good laugh.

After a while, I stopped talking to Jen. And after a few months, I noticed I didn't see her around the hospital at all. Of course, it was a huge place, so I figured she probably was transferred to another wing or something. It was always difficult for me to separate myself from a girl. I never actually told women I didn't want to see them again. I just slowly (or sometimes quickly) stopped communicating and hoped they'd get the message. I didn't have it in me to look a woman in the eye and tell her I wasn't interested anymore.

Most of my time with Vic was spent in the hospital, making rounds or tending to patients. I idolized Vic; he was like a hero to me. He represented so much of what I aspired to be. One time we were tending to a patient and had to quickly draw blood. I was on one side taking blood out, and he was on the other; we were like two bees working in tandem.

"Hey, Joe, we got a little intramural competition here," Vic said with a smile. I always appreciated his sense of humor and how even-keeled he was.

Vic and I occasionally took a drive to different areas of LA. Usually it was in the more urban areas, but one spring day Vic said we'd take a longer drive and he took me out to Pacific Palisades. I had never been there before and I'll never forget driving along Sunset and into a quaint coastal town. Driving by the manicured shopping centers, beautiful homes along tree-lined streets, and seeing the ocean in the distance, it dawned on me that this was the place to be. It was like living in the country and having it all – you were in the hills over the ocean, with quick access to town, but removed enough to feel like you were home.

"Vic, this little town is something else," I told him. Vic was calm, unimpressed. Surely he'd driven through a hundred times.

"It's a nice place," he agreed.

"It's not just nice; it's like a movie scene," I countered. Vic chuckled at me and kept driving, charismatic and collected as Cary Grant.

"Really, this place…it's the living end," I said as I continued goggling at the town and dreaming about living in one of its beautiful homes.

CHAPTER 17

The Perfect Woman

My buddy John and I were heading out on the town after a long day of work, doing our usual bar crawl, looking for women and a good time. I parked my convertible and got out, admiring my new two door Mercedes, which was actually used, but new to me. John and I were headed to a singles party at the Biltmore, a luxury hotel in downtown LA.

Approaching the door, John and I noticed a group of attractive young women looking in through the window, apparently disappointed. I walked up behind them, with John, a rather shy guy, lagging behind me. I sped up, noticing the girls were backing away from the door.

"Aren't you going in?" I said to the group as a whole. The girls turned around and one of them instantly caught my eye.

"No, I don't think so…" the gorgeous blond said. "It seems to be mostly older people."

"Nonsense! This place is great fun. You gotta come in!" I encouraged them, really just talking to the one woman.

"I don't know," another woman said, turning to investigate the party scene. I peered into the window and understood her concern. Most of the people inside seemed to be bald men.

"Tell you what. I'm a regular here. I'll introduce you to some friends and make you all comfortable. What do you say?" I said, trying to put on my most charming smile.

"Alright, I suppose we can check it out?" the blond asked her friends.

"Your choice – you're the birthday girl!" one of her friends replied encouragingly.

"It's your birthday?" I asked her.

"It is," she said with a demure smile.

"Let's go celebrate! I'll get us a round," I shouted as I pulled the door open and gestured for them to follow me. They walked in, with the birthday girl going in last. I waited for the others to pass by so I could speak with her.

"What's your name?" she asked me.

"I'm Joe. And who do I have the pleasure of speaking with?" I replied, keeping my manners in mind.

"I'm Pat. It's a pleasure to meet you."

"The pleasure is all mine. What do you drink?" I went up to the bar and ordered a round for Pat and her friends. I was instantly enamored with Pat. Her blond hair, perfect body, and sparkling blue eyes captivated me. So did her intelligence. Tonight was her twenty-first birthday and she and her friends were just about to graduate from their nursing program.

People were starting to dance and some of her friends started to partner off with other guys. "Will you dance with me?" I asked.

"Yes," she replied.

"Alright, let's go!" I exclaimed, setting down my finished drink and taking her hand. I spun her around on the dance floor to one of my favorite Sinatra songs.

"You like Sinatra?" I asked her.

"Of course."

"He's my favorite," I said, relieved she appreciated Sinatra.

"What do you do in Los Angeles, Joe? I can tell you're not from here," she said with a laugh.

"I'm a movie producer," I replied without really thinking. "I'm from Jersey, as you might have guessed."

"A movie producer?" she inquired.

"Yeah. Gotta love show business!" I said. "Did you grow up here?" I asked, changing the subject.

"I did. In the Valley."

"A Valley girl. Sounds fun," I said as I spun her around again.

We continued to dance for a long time. As the night wore on to an end, some of her friends said they had to go soon and asked if she was ready.

"I can drive you home if you'd like to stay longer," I said.

She hesitated. "You guys can go on without me. I'll have Joe drop me off," she told her friends. They said their goodbyes and then Pat and I were alone again.

On the drive home, I realized I needed to clear something up with Pat. "So, it's pretty common for nurses to be chasing after doctors, right?"

"I don't know, is it?" she replied quizzically.

"Oh, yeah," I said emphatically, thinking of all the nurses I had dated over the years. "Well, I have to tell you something. I know that because I'm actually a doctor." I paused, looking at the road ahead, waiting for her to respond. "I'm in residency."

"Oh," she said, a little puzzled. "Why did you make up that you were a producer?"

"Well, Hollywood is exciting. I've always kind of wanted to be a part of it," I admitted. "I have a lot of friends in the business."

"Being a doctor is a very admirable profession," she said hesitantly, seeming skeptical about my earlier bluff.

"I love it. I love practicing medicine."

"We seem to have a lot in common. I love being a nurse. And Hollywood excites me too," she admitted. I was relieved she seemed to let my earlier blunder slide.

I got Pat's number when I dropped her off and drove home with a smile on my face, wondering when I could see her next.

Not many dates went by before I asked Pat to marry me. We were engaged within a month. Many of my friends were surprised to see me settling down, but everything was wonderful in the relationship. She seemed to be the perfect woman and I was worried I would lose her if I did not propose. Pat had it all: She was gorgeous, intelligent, virtuous, big hearted, and had a steady job. She could have had anyone she wanted, so I figured I needed to make a commitment quickly.

The first few months of the engagement were blissful, but as the wedding crept up, I began to get cold feet. I wondered if I were too young to commit myself to marriage. There were still things that I wanted to do, like travel to Italy so I could see where my family came from.

I worked incredibly hard to make it as a doctor. I should have gone and traveled a bit after my residency, but I was insecure and figured I needed to start working. What I actually wanted more than anything else, career-wise, was to get my fellowship in hematology – which is the study of blood diseases – or cardiology, since I was a natural for it. Although I loved working with patients and helping people, the most exciting part of medicine was studying it and exploring the science behind it. If I continued on the fellowship and research track, I could potentially become a professor as well.

When I shared this goal with my mom, she was clearly disappointed. After an uncomfortable silence on the phone, she said, "Joeyyyy," in her soft, pleading, slightly belittling tone. "Enough is enough. How many years have you been in school?"

Only in retrospect did I realize how much I truly wanted to be an academic, a professor. I imagine that dream was cultivated during my time researching and studying under Father Luyet and Sister Mary. But I'd never told my mom I wanted to be an academic doctor. I'm not sure she even knew what that was. As far as she was concerned, I'd be a family doctor with a steady, admirable income.

"You're right, Ma," I said, a bit deflated. I needed to be able to support us both. She had done so much for me my entire life and I was making her proud by becoming a doctor. But pride won't pay the bills, so I let go of my desire to do a fellowship and applied for jobs.

I was in love with a wonderful woman and embarking on my medical career. I ended up getting my first job as a house doctor at a small hospital called St. Vincent. This hospital also happened to be where Pat worked.

The Wedding

Right after our two day honeymoon, I was making rounds when a nurse caught me off guard by saying, "Dr. Turcillo, you'd better come up to your office for a minute." Usually in an emergency, I was being called out of my office, not into it. As I approached my door, I heard what sounded like my mom (who was still on her visit) and my wife screaming at each other. Hoping I was wrong, I opened the door to see my mom and wife of three days in the middle of a huge argument.

"Calm down! What's going on?" I said. "Ma, Pat and I are at work." After talking to them for a few minutes, it appeared the problem was that my mom was afraid she was losing her son; she was upset we got married so quickly. I took my mom back to the house and tried to reassure her that I would always take care of her.

Later that night, I attempted to assuage Pat's concerns. At one point, she was crying, talking about how she couldn't tell if I was happy we were married. I didn't know what to say.

"Why did you marry me?" she asked through tears. I had no answer. What could I tell her? I wasn't sure if I was in love, but the gifts were in and I couldn't say no? And that was the truth; I just didn't have the guts to say no. But I couldn't tell her that.

Although Pat and I rarely fought, she and my mother could really give it to each other. Her visits were often fraught with tension and the fight in the hospital wasn't the first. I remember one particularly bad fight that kept escalating to a point where I heard Pat hurling insults at my mother, who could barely defend herself, given her limited use of English. I'd been reading and trying to ignore their argument, but I was furious with the last things Pat had said, so I walked out from the other room and found myself standing at the bottom of the stairs, looking up at them as they fought. I was about to interrupt but was glad I didn't, because just after being insulted, my mother stared at Pat and eventually grabbed her. For a split second, I was worried she might smack her or shake her, but my mother simply hugged her. Pat seemed a bit startled to find herself in my mom's arms and quieted down. And that ended the fight. Pleasantly surprised, I figured I'd let them resolve anything else on their own that night, and returned to my reading.

I was thankful that Pat and I got along well, though. We seemed to understand each other intuitively. We both loved being social but also gave each other ample space, as we both are the type of people who need some time alone to decompress. Much of our time together was spent out at dinner or at friends' parties. We always enjoyed each other's company. But given our hectic jobs, our time together was sparse. Pat seemed fine with that, though – she was incredibly independent and did not ask much of me, so I tried my best to give her everything she asked for. Between my budding career and my beautiful wife, I had it made, but lacked the life experience to realize it.

It wasn't long before Pat got pregnant. Before our first child was born, I hadn't thought much about whether or not I wanted kids. That changed the moment I held our baby Lisa in my hands – I was overcome with a sort of love I didn't know existed. I loved her instantly. In a moment our bond was sealed and I felt an overwhelming need to protect her. When Pat and I drove home in the two-door Mercedes, I must have gone ten miles per hour on the freeway. This was before car seats and I felt I couldn't possibly drive slow enough.

"You can go a little faster if you want," Pat told me.

"No, no. She's so tiny," I said, looking at our six-pound baby in Pat's arms. We smiled at each other and I continued to slowly make my way home.

Lisa looked just like me – the same dark eyes, hair, and skin. Everyone would instantly see she was my kid. When Pat walked her around in a stroller, people would ask if she was her babysitter. "No, she's my baby," she would say with slight irritation. I guess my Italian genes just overpowered Pat's blond hair, blue-eyed Irish genes.

Lisa and Me

CHAPTER 18

House Hunt

I'VE LIKED HOUSES EVER SINCE I was little. I remember how I frequently went over to my cousin's house and played in a deserted lot next door. There were all these broken bricks lying around and I sat there, putting them together, creating little playhouses. I've always been interested in houses, for whatever reason, perhaps the security they seem to give.

Once I had earned enough money to do so, I wanted to bring my mother out to California. She enjoyed living in New Jersey, but we missed each other and I wanted to be able to care for her better and keep an eye on her health.

There I was, making I think $350 per month as a resident at County, which was unheard of richness for me. When I was an intern it was only $65 per month. I thought *$350, are you crazy!* I felt like a millionaire. So once I settled down with my wife, I saw this house on Pester Avenue in Sherman Oaks; I was just driving by on my commute, saw it, and bought it later that day. It had a front house and a back house, so I figured we could live in front and my mom could live in the back house and be nearby. I explained what it was like over the phone but she wasn't very interested.

As time went on, I bought several more houses, but my mom would always say something that would make me buy another house – there was always some reason the property wasn't right. I wondered how a woman who had spent her life in cold water flats could be so picky. I bought another one in Sherman Oaks near Fashion Square.

I was in the mode of being like a squirrel, gathering things to save up for a hard time. I saw homes as security, an investment, and had great fun buying them. After buying the second Sherman Oaks home, I flew my mom out to present it to her. She walked in, looked around, and said, "This house is too big for me."

"Really? Why? You've lived in tiny apartments all your life. I wanted to get you something nicer!" I exclaimed, slightly frustrated.

"Joey, I don't need something so big. Smaller is better."

Then I bought another house near my office in Burbank. A beautiful place, like those houses in Germany, up in the hills. Nice pool. Great community. I bought it and my mother said, "Oh no, the house is in the hills. I can't live in the hills." I bought another house in the Valley. She didn't like that one either. Then I bought a condominium in Malibu. The condo wasn't my mom's taste and she said it was too cold in Malibu.

"What?" I practically yelled. "You have lived in the snow for years!"

"I want to live in the Valley near you if I move across country," she stated.

I kept buying different homes; I believe I bought nine or ten houses before getting her to move out to California. If I had kept all those places, it would have been an incredible investment.

At the time, I thought my mom was being difficult. I later realized that she knew what she was doing the whole time: She was trying to get me to invest and to keep my money in safe places, so I wouldn't spend it all on useless activities or fancy cars. She couldn't read or write, but she knew what she was doing. As many years have gone by and I've watched my properties appreciate, I'm very thankful that my mom's plan incentivized me to buy several houses. The moral of the story is to take good care of your mother and to listen to your mother.

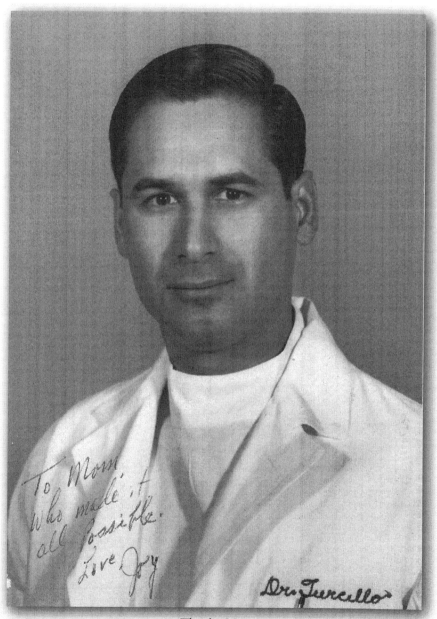

Thanks, Mom

CHAPTER 19

Locked In

IN THE SIXTIES, WHILE WORKING at LA County General, I received a panicked call from my friend Regina. She was a true alpha woman: shrewd and brilliant, you didn't dare cross her.

I picked up the phone and before I could say anything, I heard a panicked woman ask, "Joe, would you do me a favor? Rick is in a coma at a Beverly Hills hospital—"

"—What happened?" I interrupted. Her husband Rick was a young, successful baseball player. He was a vibrant tour-de-force in his early thirties. It seemed like nothing could touch him.

"He went to the dentist two days ago. Then yesterday, he went blind for a few minutes. I called the dentist and he said to take some aspirin," Regina quickly explained.

My heart sank as I heard this. I instantly knew what was wrong. "It sounds like he has a brain abscess. I'll head over to him now." I didn't tell Regina this yet, but if my diagnosis was right, her husband was likely terminal.

As I rushed down to my car, I shook my head at the thought of the dentist who had told him to take an aspirin. If someone goes *blind*, even if it's only temporary, he should call his doctor immediately. That's just common sense. Why a dentist – a profession requiring an advanced scientific degree – would be so flippant was beyond me. Had Regina called me, I would have demanded that she rush Rick to the ER right away.

Arriving at his hospital room, I nodded at Regina and got to work. Rick was, of course, comatose. His neurologist was there and briefed me on the situation. His analysis was that Rick was probably suffering from a postictal state (which is the distorted state of consciousness after a seizure).

"Are you crazy?" I almost yelled out. "He probably has a brain abscess. We've got to get him in surgery."

The neurosurgeon was surprised but I explained my theory: that Rick had subacute bacterial endocarditis (SBE). This condition occurs when an infection goes from the teeth to the heart, then spreads throughout the body. It is rare and extremely dangerous, but I had seen it in residency so I was able to identify it. The situation also made sense, as Rick went blind after having dental work. His neurosurgeon agreed that SBE was quite probable, so we sent Rick in to surgery.

Rick was operated on by two neurosurgeons I respected at a neighboring hospital. They were brothers named John and Evan. As they operated on Rick, I was there to observe and advise. They had his head open and were probing around, telling me they didn't see anything abnormal. Nevertheless, I was convinced that if they kept digging, they would find evidence of a brain abscess.

"We still don't see anything here," John said as he worked away on Rick's brain.

"Go deeper," I urged them.

We didn't have CAT scans in those days, so the only way to know for sure if he had a brain abscess was to open him up. I would not have advocated for this unless I had been extremely confident in my diagnosis.

"Still nothing..." Evan said without looking up, still examining Rick's brain.

"Go deeper," I insisted again. One of them let out a sigh as they continued. A few quiet minutes went by as I tentatively watched their tedious work.

"Ta-da," said Evan, breaking the silence with a little inappropriate humor. "We've hit a puss pocket." I sighed, feeling slight relief that we hadn't opened him up unnecessarily, but also had a sinking feeling that the infection had probably spread throughout the body, which would mean Rick was terminal. All the surgeons could do at the time was drain the puss out of his brain and administer antibiotics.

After the surgery, Regina insisted that I continuously check on Rick. SBE was a rare condition and though I felt fairly certain the infection had spread and would cause Rick to die, we would not know if it had spread until after he died; we needed an autopsy to be certain.

Regina wouldn't stop talking to me as I looked after her husband. Her incessant discussion was frustrating because I had this eerie sense that, although he was in a coma, Rick was aware of what was going on. I felt as if he could hear us and was in an incredible amount of pain, but could not move or communicate. Of course, I did not tell his wife that, because my belief was based on an inexplicable intuition. At that time, I had no scientific evidence to back it up. There was just a palpable sense that this man was suffering and that his brain was working even as his body remained paralyzed.

Given my strong feeling that Rick had no hope and was probably suffering, I did not want to keep him alive if there was no hope of survival. As his wife talked to me endlessly, I couldn't help but think "Please lady, please stop talking to me. Please stop me from aggressively keeping him alive." I wouldn't do anything in contrast to her wishes, and that was to continue aggressive treatment, so I continued to keep him alive as long as I could.

Weeks went by and each day I would visit Rick, or his comatose body, rather. Naturally, all of Rick's youthful energy and exuberance for life was gone and after a while I wouldn't have recognized him if I hadn't been treating him all along. It was heart wrenching to see this previously young, athletic, genuinely kind man hanging between life and death.

Any care was to no avail and Rick died after about a month of treatment. This came as no shock – actually, it was a relief because I knew it was inevitable and if he had been suffering, at least his anguish was over. I had visited him every day since his admission but there was nothing I (or anyone else) could have done to change the course of his illness.

When the autopsy was completed, we confirmed he had SBE and also found he had a predisposition to the condition. His aortic valve, what we call the bicuspid valve, was incredibly liable to get infections because instead of a typical trivalve, it was a bivalve. Having a bivalve gives someone a far higher chance of SBE. The autopsy showed he had an infection throughout the body, meaning all his medical care had been hopeless.

As knowledge about SBE progressed, we later learned that Rick was in what we call a locked-in syndrome (LIS). It's a horrible death because although the patient cannot move, he is aware of what's going on. And recently we have learned that the only way these people can communicate is by movement of their eyes – either up or down. The eye is the only voluntary muscle that isn't paralyzed in LIS. But we didn't know that at the time. I somehow just knew Rick was aware, for whatever reason. This case has always stuck with me because of the sudden turn of health and the suffering my young patient endured in his last days.

CHAPTER 20

The Dixie Cup

———

Two years after Lisa was born, we had our second daughter, Susie, in 1967. I loved her instantly, just as I had bonded with Lisa. I had very little time with them, though, as I was still in the early years of establishing my private practice.

Lisa was running around by the time Susie was born and I would often lift her up and hug her so much that she would get a bit irritated; I just couldn't get enough of her. I called my kids my cubs because I felt like a bear with its cubs – protecting them, providing for them, and playing with them. As long as I was with them, the world was fine. All I truly cared about was that I had them. Susie appeared to reflect more of her mother's qualities – she was quiet, introspective, incredibly kind, and independent – while Lisa seemed to have more of a temperament like mine – fun-loving, energetic, boisterous. She also had a serious side. Even as a toddler, Lisa looked dignified; sometimes you'd forget she was four until she spoke and you were reminded she was a child. One time, over dinner, Lisa said she wanted more food. Pat got up to add more chicken to her plate and I jokingly said, "Give her the bones, Pat."

Lisa looked at me in all seriousness, with a bit of defiance and announced, "Don't want bones. Want meat." Pat and I laughed and Susie started giggling too, imitating us. Lisa stared at me in frustration until I told her we were only kidding and that she could have more chicken. Unfortunately, family dinners like that didn't happen very often.

Pat and I also did our own thing most of the time – usually out of circumstance, due to our work schedules. We were both independent. As time went by, other women caught my eye. Where I grew up, married men often had a woman (or women) on the side and their wives looked the other way; that was the norm.

Pat

Driving to an event with Vic one night, I reflected on my good fortune. "You know, Vic, I got it pretty good. Pat is beautiful, has a good job, she cooks, she makes love to me, and she doesn't get on my case about things. And she doesn't ask me where I've been when I come home at two or three in the morning. I have captain's paradise!" I said, referring to the film about a sailor with two wives, each in a different port. "I'd never leave her."

Pat would wait for me to come home and I would tell her I had to work late. Sometimes I truly was working to the early morning hours, in the ER with patients, but other times I was out on the town. I'm not sure why, but she never complained. Much later, I found out that other people told her I was running around, but she did not believe it until her best friend told her we had slept together. At that point, Pat told me to leave. I never would have left her, but she told me to get out. So I left.

The divorce was ugly. I suppose it must be for most couples, especially if they have children. We fought and hired lawyers. Looking back, I wish we could have done it differently. Of course, I wish I had done so much differently as a husband and father. I did not know what I had in life. If I could do it again, I would be the best husband and father. I would be Prince Charming to Pat and far more involved in the kids' lives. As the saying goes, we learn too late in life.

Pat got custody of the kids for most of the time. I could visit on weekends. I loved our time playing together. I often took them to see friends at Sunday gatherings. It was nice to have them in groups because, to be frank, I was unaware of how to care for them when they were very small. It's ironic that I was a doctor and took care of people for a living, but never formally learned anything about raising children. Of course, few people do – they learn it from family and friends. And I didn't truly take on the responsibility to learn how to care for young kids, which I regret. I also think it's a shame that, as a society, we aren't taught how to care for children.

The most painful part of visiting the kids was when I took them back to Pat's. I'll never forget the first time I had to do that. Lisa was four and Susie was two. After I said goodbye and turned around, Lisa cried, "Daddy! Daddy! Don't go!" and Susie followed her, also crying. Lisa ran to my leg, tugging at it, pleading for me to stay. That happened over and over again. Each time I was reminded of when my father was taken away from me and I clung to his leg in tears.

I felt horrible about the divorce for the kids' sake. I moved to a home in Burbank very close to Pat's, so that I could be near them. It was crucial to me that the family wasn't completely torn apart. Fortunately, the kids also had their Aunt Susan, Pat's sister (who Susie was named after) with them in the early years. After the divorce, Susan moved in to help Pat – who still had a demanding job – take care of them.

Between Pat and her sister, the kids had the most attention. The two sisters would dress them up like dolls and take them out for walks, with people stopping to admire the adorable babies. On Halloween, they always outdid themselves and created crazy costumes for the kids. Most of the time, when

I saw the pictures, I was very impressed by their craftsmanship, but unsure what the kids were supposed to be dressed as.

Depending on how things were going, sometimes Pat wouldn't allow me in her house at all. During one of these periods, Lisa had broken her arm doing gymnastics and I wanted to leave her a gift to cheer her up. I bought her a giant stuffed animal, a rabbit, and tried to figure out how I'd get it in the house. Finally I realized I could squeeze it through the doggy door. It barely fit, but I got it through and then positioned it next to the door, hoping she'd notice it once she got home.

Given how demanding my work and dating life were, I did not go on many vacations. Now that the kids were old enough that they could be away from Pat for a little while, I decided it was time for a family vacation. I had the brilliant idea that we should go to New Jersey to see my mother, Lou, and the rest of the gang. The brilliant part was that we would go by train.

I figured it would be an unforgettable opportunity for the kids and me to go cross-country together. This way, we would see so much more than we could ever view from a plane. I was also terrified of flying.

Although I was slightly afraid of flying most of my life, I only developed a true fear after Lou and I were on a flight to Vegas. We were a ways into the flight when I looked out my window and saw smoke coming from the back of the plane.

"Hey, Lou," I said nervously, nudging him.

"What, Joe?" he asked flatly, annoyed to be interrupted from reading a physics book.

"Look at the smoke!" I exclaimed. Lou looked out and shot me a look of concern. Just then, the announcement warning dinged.

"Ladies and gentlemen, this is your pilot" a calm voice announced. "You may have noticed that the engine is on fire, so we'll need to land the plane now." A sense of panic swept the plane and a few people who hadn't seen the smoke screamed.

"Noticed!" I practically yelled. Noticed! Yeah, we sure as hell noticed there is smoke coming from the back of the plane. The pilots were able to do a safe, unplanned landing at another airport, where we got on another plane going toward Vegas. But ever since then, I tried to avoid flying whenever I could. Even if it meant taking a train across the country.

"Are you sure this is a good idea? Can you really handle them for that long?" Pat asked me the day before our train trip.

"Are you kidding me? Of course I can!" I replied confidently. I genuinely thought it would be a pretty seamless trip.

"Alright," Pat conceded.

The next day I arrived at Pat's and scooped my girls up, carrying a kid in each arm.

"Daddy! Daddy!" they squealed, with laughter and big smiles.

"We're going on a big adventure today, girls!" I exclaimed. Pat raised an eyebrow in concern.

Once the train was pulling out, I looked at our cramped cabin and wondered how we were going to make it for three days on the train. I estimated it was about 12" x 7" and I had to hunch over so that I wouldn't hit the ceiling while walking around. I pushed the concern from my mind, remembering that this would be a delightful trip.

Needless to say, I was in over my head. After dinner, I knew the kids needed to wash up. How was I going to wash the kids? I wondered. I had not considered this issue while planning the trip. Susie had been crawling all over the floor in the dining car – there was no way around it: She needed a bath.

Lisa looked on as I tried to wash Susie in our incredibly small sink. Susie was a good sport as I used a Dixie cup to pour water onto her, then lathered her with some soap, and rinsed her off by repeatedly pouring the Dixie cup. Once I finished I looked at Lisa and said, "Well, kid. Your turn." I lifted her into the sink and washed her in the same ridiculous way.

By the time we rolled into Chicago, I grabbed the kids and our suitcase and rushed off the train. "We're flying the rest of the way, kids!" I announced. Though flying on airplanes was something I almost always avoided, I figured it would be more bearable than continuing all the way to New Jersey by train.

Once the plane took off, I was already a couple of drinks in and let out a sigh of relief. The woman sitting next to me asked me about the kids and I explained the situation.

"Wow, you tried to take them all the way across the country?" she said with her eyebrows raised in surprise.

"Yes. What a fool I was," I said and finished my drink, setting it down dramatically.

"You must be exhausted."

"Certainly. And I don't like to fly…hence the drinks," I said, raising my cup for an imaginary toast. She laughed a little.

"Your girls are so beautiful."

"Aren't they? I just love them to bits, these rascals," I said as I patted Lisa on the head. "They sure have been a challenge the past few days, though. Susie cut herself on her chin when she was running around on the platform…" I went off about the various trials we had on our train ride, including the Dixie cup baths.

"Oh, you poor thing," she said playfully. "Well, I love children. Can I play with them once they can get up and run around?" she asked.

"Please do!" I pleaded.

Fortunately, the kind woman next to me ended up being a nurse and was flying with a few friends. They took pity on me and adopted the kids and me for the flight. They started playing with the girls once we were in the air. Knowing the kids were being taken care of, I readily accepted when the stewardess offered me another drink. I instantly threw it back and accepted a few more, eventually getting stoned drunk.

Shortly after that ill-fated trip, I eventually convinced my mother to move out to California. After all the houses she had me buy, she ended up wanting to move in with me, and like a true Italian son, I welcomed her. She moved into my house in Pacific Palisades, a coastal town situated on a bluff between Malibu and Santa Monica that I'd fallen in love with years earlier when I drove through it with Vic. It was a great little house and a charming town, Pacific Palisades.

The happiest moments in my life were those weekend mornings at the Palisades house when I sat with Susie and Lisa at our kitchen table while my mom cooked breakfast. The kids would color and I took in the aroma of my mom's Italian cooking, talking with her and the kids. Or building airplane models with the kids. Susie was particularly mechanically minded from a very young age and loved playing with toy planes, cars, and trucks. We also loved riding our bikes to our favorite ice cream place and eating spaghetti together. Despite all the crazy and wild moments in my life, those simple moments with family are the ones I cherish most. There's nothing like spending time with your family.

CHAPTER 21

Sweet Sixteen

———

OVER THE YEARS, MANY OF my patients became friends and many of my friends became patients. This gave me confidence, because it showed that people trusted me. I always wanted to be more than a person's doctor. I wanted to be his advisor, friend, and advocate – someone he could rely on. That said, sometimes I was asked to advise on matters that seemed completely out of my field. Certain patients grew accustomed to asking my advice, even on things that had nothing to do with medicine. Sometimes it would be questions about relationship advice (which I could offer opinions on) or even legal advice (which I never dared to touch).

On a busy day, between many appointments and hospital visits, I got a call from Mrs. Weaver, a woman I'd met in passing at the hospital. She explained that she was concerned about her daughter's dating life; she was seeing an "older boy" and was having "boy trouble." The girl's schoolwork was being affected. Although I was quite confused about why she was confiding in me – an internist who specialized in heart and lung issues – I listened patiently.

It became clear that, as a highly moral Irish woman, Mrs. Weaver's biggest concern was whether or not her daughter was sexually active. From what she said, it seemed she was unable, or perhaps unwilling, to find this out from her daughter directly. In that time, it was common for families to seek out a priest or doctor for guidance or even intervention. I'd never been asked to intervene about something like this before, though.

"I'm happy to see her if you'd like," I said slowly, "but I mostly see geriatric patients and I don't have any experience with counseling in this area. You might be better off with…a psychotherapist, perhaps."

"I'd like you to see her. You're a heart specialist and I trust you," she said.

The whole scenario seemed odd to me but Mrs. Weaver was quite insistent. She booked an appointment and I forgot about the conversation until I looked up from my desk to see her sixteen year-old daughter a few days later. I guess I had expected a teen that looked more, well, rebellious. Perhaps she'd be a hippy with a button that read "make love not war" or an angst-riddled type with a tortured countenance. But the girl standing in front of me couldn't have looked more wholesome. She had a clear complexion, beautiful eyes, long blonde hair, and crisp, conservative clothes. I looked at my chart and saw her name was Sharon.

Thinking back to my conversation with her mother, it dawned on me that her mom might have thought that a heart doctor could help fix matters of the heart and I wanted to laugh, but remained professional. Regardless of her reasoning, I knew that Mrs. Weaver would still want me to make sure Sharon wasn't sleeping with her boyfriend.

Sharon and I got to talking and I explained there were concerns about her romantic life. She was cooperative and pleasant as I began asking some personal questions. I quickly confirmed that she had an older boyfriend, who was actually a full-grown twenty-four year old man. No wonder her mother was concerned, I thought. As a doctor, I had to make sure she was being safe.

"Do the two of you make love?" I asked.

She blushed and quietly replied, "Yes."

"Do you use protection?" I checked.

"No," she replied. I was surprised. She seemed like a responsible girl. But then again, maybe she hadn't been educated in this matter. Clearly, her mother was a bit confused, thinking that a heart specialist could help solve her daughter's romance problems.

"Aren't you afraid of getting pregnant?" I quickly replied, gearing up for a speech on safe sex.

"No," she said quietly. "We make love, but not like *that*."

Stumped, I asked, "Well, how do you make love then?"

She blushed even more now, looking down and not wanting to meet my eyes, she replied, "We kiss a lot, but that's all."

To be thorough, I asked, "So you're not sexually active...you're still a virgin?"

"Of course."

I burst out laughing at the situation and our misunderstandings.

Looking stunned and embarrassed, she tentatively asked, "Why are you laughing?"

With a light heart and a smile I replied, "Your mom sent you here because she thought you had heart issues. I had no idea what she meant by that, but I'm just realizing she must have thought your romantic issues were literally related to your heart." Sharon stared back at me. "And besides," I added, "you have to be the most refreshing person I've ever met! You're so innocent. You really are sweet sixteen...in every way."

She smiled back at me and seemed relieved. "That is why my mom sent me," she confirmed. "I figured she had already explained that to you. I thought it was odd that she wanted me to come here, but she was adamant."

Thinking of her worried mother, I asked, "Sharon, is it alright with you if I tell your mother you're not sexually active?"

"Yes, of course," she replied. A look of relief washed over her face as she seemed to realize her mother would be pleased with the results.

It occurred to me that I should give Sharon some relationship and life advice. Borrowing a line from President Truman, I told her to "Give 'em hell." She smiled and sat back, appearing to take my suggestion into consideration.

Looking at the teenager before me, I was struck by how youthful and energetic she was – a stark contrast to the geriatric patients I saw day to day. I rarely interacted with young people other than my children and virtually never had young patients. I loved all my patients, but it was refreshing to see someone just beginning her life, as opposed to someone at the tail end of it. Feeling more comfortable now that the big question was out of the way, I leaned back in my chair, clasping my hands behind my head and asked Sharon more about her life. When I first met a patient, I always tried to make time to get to know them on a personal level. I always thought this was important, to build trust and rapport. Naturally, I spoke with some patients at more length than others, depending on how much we had in common and how social they were.

It was the end of the day and she was waiting for her mom to pick her up anyway, so I spent a while talking to Sharon. We got to discussing a number of topics, from literature to movies to cars to restaurants. Above all, I found it surprising that we could have so many similar interests and feel so in sync, despite the twenty-year age difference. I thought to myself that I wished more teenagers could be like Sharon – what a more pleasant world we'd live in. It was remarkable to meet such a young person who was so inquisitive and intellectual.

As we wrapped up, I closed her chart and scratched "no charge" on the slip. Over time I got to know her parents better and we became friends. I wouldn't see Sharon again until two years later, when I went to watch her graduate from high school with honors.

Just a year before watching Sharon graduate, I'd gone to my own twenty-year high school reunion. I was a fresh divorcee with two toddlers by then. Although I'd been back home many times to see my buddies and my family, there were many people from high school that I hadn't seen since graduation. I wanted to do more than simply show up at the reunion, so I hosted a party the night before at Barcelona's Bar & Grill, the Italian joint where I spent so much of my youth. Word quickly got around that I was hosting and many people I didn't even recognize showed up, until there were over thirty people there.

At the party, I met some vaguely familiar looking women. It took me a few minutes to place them but suddenly I realized that they were the cheerleaders I used to dream about dating in high school. I thought back to my sixteen-year-old self, when I'd first seen them and how I never mustered the courage to talk to them. With a sense of relief, I realized I wasn't nervous anymore. After all, I was building a successful career and felt I had a lot to be proud of. The women and I hit it off and before the night wore to an end, I suggested they come visit me in Los Angeles. They enthusiastically took me up on the offer, which was a pleasant surprise.

A few months later I was giving the cheerleaders the grand LA tour, from the Hollywood Walk of Fame to the beaches in Malibu. Finally, I admitted how I used to always want to talk to them in high school, but that I didn't think they'd give me the time of day; they seemed too preoccupied with the football players. With genuine surprise, one of them responded, "But Joe, we never even knew you existed. If only you'd told us!"

CHAPTER 22

Singing In The Porsche

I ALWAYS ENJOYED SURPRISING THE kids in different ways. One day I bought a megaphone and pulled up to Pat's to pick up the kids for the weekend. Instead of ringing the doorbell, I pulled out the megaphone, cleared my throat, and my voice boomed as I emphatically announced, "Lisa, Susie! Your dad is here!" A few seconds later, the front door flew open and the kids came running out, giggling, wanting to play with the megaphone. Even Pat seemed to briefly laugh before slightly shaking her head at me.

She may have said something like, "You're definitely different, Joe," before she passed the children off to me. Then we hopped in the car and I asked them what singer they wanted to listen to. Susie was still too small to decide but Lisa excitedly made a suggestion. Of course, she only had a few options, because back then we had an eight track in the car and there were only so many artists I carried, anyway. What the kids and I loved most, though, was that my car had an outlet for a microphone, so we could sing and have our own voices belt out of the stereo. All three of us vied for more time on the microphone, the kids often grabbing it from each other to have a solo during their favorite parts of a song.

Our favorite song to sing together was "Hi Lili, Hi Lo" from the movie *Lili*, which happens to be my favorite film. It begins with a rather sweet tune, one that sounds fairly happy. And the singer begins, singing all the while in a cheerful voice, but the lyrics are quite somber on their own. Nevertheless, we sang it with exuberant happiness, belting out the lines: "A song of love is a sad song / Hi-li Hi-lili Hi-lo / A song of love is a song of woe / Don't ask me how I know / A song of love is a sad song / For I have loved and it's so."

My favorite song to sing solo was "When You Wish Upon A Star," from *Pinocchio.* That song breaks my heart; I got completely immersed in songs like that. But if I had the mic too long, one of the girls was sure to insist that it was her turn to sing and I'd pass it along. I taped recordings of us singing together and stored them away so that I could relive those moments with the kids when they got older. In case they ever contested how much fun I was, I could replay the recordings and they'd hear their young selves announce, "This is Lisa and Susie. We're here with Daddy, riding in the Porsche!"

Susie in pigtails

Usually my weekends with the kids were spent doing family activities, but occasionally I'd have to be at a conference. When the kids were about three and five, I had a conference at St. Joseph Hospital that I couldn't get out of, so I asked one of my favorite nuns if she could watch them. Sister Claire was happy to look after them for a few hours.

About halfway through the day, Sister Claire came into the auditorium to get me.

"Susie won't stop crying, Joe...when you have a moment, can you come check on her?"

"What's the matter?"

"She misses you."

I stepped out with Sister Claire in order to check on Susie. Walking over, she told me that Susie had been yelling "I want my daddy!" over and over again and that at one point, my daughter even evaded her and ran off. The poor nun went chasing Susie all over until she was eventually able to corner her in the bathroom and haul her back over to the waiting room.

"Lisa's been very pleasant to watch, but we can't get Susie to calm down," she added.

I apologized for the difficulty and was surprised to see Susie still crying when I opened the door.

"Daddy!" she yelled as she ran over to me. I scooped her up and she clung tightly to my chest.

"Daddy, I missed you," she said very seriously, her face still wet with tears.

"It's okay, Susie, I was just around the corner. I have an important meeting but I'll spend the rest of the day with you and Lisa afterwards. Can you stay with Lisa and Sister Claire just for a little while longer?" Then I turned to Lisa and said, "Any idea why your sister is so upset?"

Lisa shrugged and came over to us. I knelt down and gave her a hug too and asked the kids to follow Sister's direction until we could go home. As I walked back to the conference room, I thought about how resolute Susie was, like a little fighter. I assumed she got that from Pat's Irish lineage. Lisa was the same way – strong and spirited.

One time, when that fighting spirit was channeled into a tantrum, I got very overwhelmed. It had been a long day and I was picking the kids up from Pat's and for some reason, Lisa was very upset. She was screaming and crying over nothing and my first thought was to spank her. After all, I'd been spanked many times as a kid. But I knew I couldn't do that; I just felt it wouldn't have been right. I remember her screaming, "I want my daddy!" just like Susie had and I replied, "Lisa, I'm right here!" but she was still so upset, throwing things and crying. Instead of hitting her, I instinctively picked her up and held her tight to me. She kept crying for a few moments and finally started to calm down as I held her in my arms. And as she quieted down, I thought back to the time my mother had hugged Pat in the middle of an argument, and was thankful I'd made the same choice.

A few years after Susie's incident at the conference, I got a distressed call from Pat. The only time we talked was to coordinate things with the kids. "Joe, I'm not sure what's wrong, but she isn't learning to read."

"Sometimes it takes kids a while," I said nonchalantly. "It took me a while." I thought back to how I was held back for not knowing how to read. Pat sighed.

"This is different. You didn't have anyone at home to teach you. Susie has me – and my sister. We work with her on it a lot."

"I'm sure it's just a matter of time."

"Joe, listen to me. Something is off. Susie is very smart. She's been taking things apart and putting them back together since she was three, but there's a roadblock with the reading. She tries to learn, but it just doesn't stick."

"Well, what do you want me to do about it?" I wanted to help, but I didn't know how.

"I don't know. I'll talk to her teacher again," Pat said with concern.

Pat and Susan kept trying to teach Susie to read and eventually gained some traction, but she could not keep up with the pace of her classmates. We were perplexed as we watched our curious, mechanically minded, and focused child fall behind.

It was like we were helpless to fix it. I was busy working at my newly established private practice. I didn't know anything about learning disabilities. As Susie's problem persisted, we were all puzzled by her learning troubles. Pat suggested we send her to a tutor, which I happily paid for.

But then Pat started telling me that Susie was being made fun of in school. It's hard for any parent to hear that. But I also didn't know what to do to fix that. I kept paying the bills for anything Pat said the kids needed and focused mostly on my work. In retrospect, I wish I would have been more hands on and tried to teach her more myself. While I did spend time with the kids, it wasn't enough time. Back then, I was preoccupied by caring for my patients and dating as many women as my limited free time permitted.

CHAPTER 23

Sunset Strip

EVEN AS A DIVORCED DAD, the Sunset Strip was my stomping ground, in terms of dating. But wherever I went, I always kept an eye out for beautiful women. On a trip in Orlando, I found myself experiencing a bit of déjà vu. After a long walk through parts of the city, I stopped and waited for the traffic light in order to cross the street. Out of the corner of my eye I saw a gorgeous red Porsche with an even more gorgeous woman at the wheel. She pulled right in front of me to wait for the light, just like a girl had done in my youth. And again, I went right up to her and talked to her. I did things a bit differently this time, though.

"Take me for a ride," I said playfully.

The woman paused for a second. I couldn't quite make out her expression behind her large sunglasses. Then she broke into a smile and said, "Hop in."

As we zipped around the city, I explained that I was visiting some friends in Florida. I suggested she show me a fun part of town. She took me to a nightclub and we danced for hours. When I flew back to LA the next day, I thought back to my younger self and had to smile at the version of me who asked, "How does a guy like me meet a girl like you?"

Most of my work was with the elderly, so on my off hours, I enjoyed spending time in vibrant scenes with younger people having a good time. I found it important to have fun when I wasn't working or studying and I never had trouble finding fun. If you have money and live in a place like LA, there's no shortage of ways to entertain yourself.

Naturally, my go-to form of entertainment was going out with my friends and meeting women. Though I dated many women, most of my relationships were here today and gone tomorrow. Lou used to say that if a girl I dated lasted more than a weekend, we were in a relationship. Of course, some women were different and made me want to pursue something more serious. In 1972 I met a woman named Nancy at a party. I first saw her across the room in a gorgeous dress, with long hair and a certain air of class and confidence. When we started talking, I instantly felt a connection with her and a sort of comfort. Years later, she told me that she was drawn to me partially because she sensed some deep sadness that she wanted to nurture and heal.

Nancy was a nurse and an airline stewardess, back in the days when that was an extremely competitive job. At the time, women had to meet certain aesthetic requirements, like having a small enough waist. Naturally, these requirements didn't stand long before discrimination laws put a stop to them.

Sometimes, with certain people, things just feel easy and natural, and that's how I felt with Nancy. We dated on and off for about ten years, sometimes fighting but always finding our way back to each other. Nancy grew close to my mother and my kids and was the only woman I brought home that they all approved of.

Another thing that distinguished Nancy was that I bought her a watch. I never bought the women I was dating things like that. I was, after all, still somewhat the same guy who didn't write his mom birthday cards.

In the early seventies, I decided to buy a trailer and live in Marina Del Rey, right next to the canals and close to the airport and a fun social scene. Nancy spent most of her free time with me there and we had the most delightful times living rather simply in the trailer and going out frequently to see our friends.

It was such a fun period for other reasons, too. I was just a hop, skip and a jump from LAX, where beautiful stewardesses would fly in from all over the country. I'd pick up different stewardesses from different terminals, often in the same night. I remember running from one date to the next, picking a girl up at Terminal Three, taking her out, then dropping her back and picking up another girl at the next terminal. And sometimes, I'd go out for another date in the same night. I distinctly remember thinking to myself: I'm crazy running for my third date. Just finished seeing two girls and now I'm running – and I was literally running – to the third date.

On days when I wasn't at the hospital all hours, I would head over to the Sunset Strip after work. There was a great bar back then called Cirano's, which I came to love because I befriended the maître d', who was a good Italian guy. After some time, we became good friends and he would start lining up girls for me. He just offered easy introductions. If a girl was shy, this was a way for her to meet me.

Occasionally I'd stop by on a lunch break as well, if I had the time. One day I'm sitting there having my cappuccino and in walks a girl who looks like a Victoria's Secret model walking down the runway with her wings. The way the sun was facing at that moment, I saw her silhouette but couldn't see much of her face. And I thought: Oh my God, I wish I could have her. She's a ten-plus.

I tried not to stare but was concerned maybe I had looked a bit too long when it seemed she was staring back at me. I averted my eyes and pretended like I was focused on my newspaper and cappuccino. Yet out of the corner of my eye, I could see her coming toward me and started wondering what the hell was going to happen. And all the sudden she says, "Joe!" and I'm thinking: Are you crazy, God? Are you putting me on here?

I looked at her and wondered if she might be talking to someone else, because I had no idea who she was. The mysterious woman called my name again, saying, "Joe! Don't you know me?" Just as she finished her question, the light from the door finally dissipated and I recognized her – standing before me was one of the student nurses I had dated back in the early days of my residency.

I was speechless a moment and before I could say anything, she leaned down, cupped her hand around my ear, and whispered, "Remember when we broke the bed?"

I chuckled and said, "How could I forget that?" She sat down next to me and we got to talking. She told me she quit nursing when I ditched her and was now working as a stewardess on United Airlines.

"United?" I asked, surprised. That was the airline Nancy flew. I asked if she knew Nancy and she excitedly told me that she did – they flew the route to Hawaii together all the time. And there went any possibility of seeing Jen again. My enthusiasm about reuniting with this goddess began to wilt.

I played it out in my mind: Nancy would be showing Jen the watch I had just given her and Jen would ask about what her boyfriend was like. Jen would listen politely, then tell Nancy about the young, suave doctor she had met. And Nancy would ask some more questions about him, then suddenly it would dawn on them that they were dating the same man and Nancy would yell out, "What? That's my boyfriend!"

Clearly, I wasn't going to get away with this. Nancy's stewardess friends all knew me. One time I was boarding a flight to go to a medical seminar in Hawaii and I heard someone yell out, "Joe! What are you doing here? You're afraid to fly!" I turned around and to my surprise, it wasn't just a *passenger* pointing out my fear, but one of the flight attendants – a good friend of Nancy's.

So I didn't dare make a move. I knew when and when not to make a move, because Nancy and I were practically living together in the trailer in the Marina. But it sure was a strange coincidence to gawk at this stunning woman as she walked into the bar, then realize she had been incredibly in love with me years prior. And the fact that she now flew with Nancy only added to the strangeness of it all.

CHAPTER 24

An Unexpected Welcome

IN THE EARLY SEVENTIES, I opened an office in Burbank and hired a couple of women to do administrative work. They seemed kind enough, but I shortly saw that I had hired the wrong individuals – things were a mess. I pondered what to do but realized that although I hated firing people, I had to do what was best for my patients and myself. Suddenly, a good idea hit me: What if I hired Sharon, the girl who was sent to me at age sixteen for her "heart problems." She was smart as a whip, energetic, responsible, and majoring in business at USC. I was sure she could handle the job – maybe even by herself.

The next day I called her and told her I was interested in having her come work for me.

There was a long pause. "That's very flattering, Joe, but I'm not really looking for a job at the moment," she said politely.

"Why don't you come on down today and let me give you a tour and discuss the possibility of it. Then you could make a more informed decision," I replied.

"I suppose I could," she said reluctantly. "What time should I come in?"

Later that afternoon, I introduced Sharon as a college girl who might help with filing. Of course, this wasn't entirely true, but I figured it was the best way for Sharon to shadow the employees without making any waves. The current employees showed Sharon the ropes in a few hours, but they seemed suspicious of Sharon – as if they knew she might threaten their jobs. They knew as well as I did that things weren't being done properly. Throughout the day, as I walked in and out to see patients, I kept an eye on Sharon to see if it seemed like she might be getting the hang of things. Each time I checked, she was always busy, running around filing something away or answering a phone. It was a relief to see how much initiative she took. I desperately needed someone more organized and efficient so that I could put my full attention on my patients' medical needs.

At the end of the day, I pulled Sharon in to my office and shut the door. Lowering my voice, I asked, "Do you think you could run this place yourself?"

She looked a bit startled. After all, I had omitted the fact that I hoped she could replace not one but *both* of the current employees.

"The business doesn't need two people to run it," she replied diplomatically. I nodded, then pulled out a pair of office keys and placed them in her hand.

"Be here at nine tomorrow morning," I said with a smile and a pat on the shoulder. I walked off, leaving Sharon a bit stunned and silent. When she walked out, I watched my current employees glare at her until the door gently shut behind her. At the end of the day, I let them go, which was always an awful feeling. They both took it harder than I expected, given they had only been working there for a couple of months.

The next morning I walked in a couple of minutes after nine and was startled when I opened the door to see Sharon quickly trying to clean up the complete scene of chaos that she found upon opening that morning: Trash cans were overturned, the charts were jumbled up into unusable piles, and the lab reports were scattered all over the floor.

"What the hell!" I practically yelled. Sharon looked startled.

"It was like this when I came in, Dr. Turcillo," she said a bit timidly. "The second I turned on the lights a few minutes ago, it was just a complete mess."

"I guess I upset them more than I thought," I muttered, rubbing my head.

"What happened? Did you already fire them?" she asked.

"Yes." I could see that Sharon was surprised that the women were let go so quickly. "You said it should only take one person to run the office..." She simply looked at me, wide eyed.

"I should have seen them out and locked up myself," I said.

"Well, I'm going to clean this up as much as I can. Do you have an appointment book? So I can figure out who is coming in today..." she trailed off.

"Yes, of course. It's the black book that they usually keep right next to the phone," I said as I pointed to where I had always seen it, then suddenly noticed it wasn't there.

"Oh, shit. Where did they put it?" I said, feeling a new wave of anxiety creep in. We frantically began looking for it. Without the appointment book, we wouldn't know who was coming in and when. Naturally, it's important to know what's already been booked for scheduling purposes, but it's also necessary so that you can prepare the right charts ahead of time. If we couldn't find the appointment book, we'd be partially in the dark for the rest of the year... and it was only February.

My head started to ache just thinking about it. Sharon could see my distress and suggested that I get prepared to see patients, although we had no idea who was coming in that day. I took her advice, sensing it would be better to let her get organized on her own. After all, she was the expert there and organizing was never my forte.

We improvised for the rest of the day. When a patient came in, I stalled things by chatting unusually long with them. This was easy for me to do because I loved my patients and they loved me as well. Some of the more friendly ones particularly seemed to enjoy how long we exchanged small talk while I was waiting for Sharon to find and prep their charts. Once she brought them in, I could commence with the evaluation.

We were in for another surprise, however, at the end of the day when I was going to show Sharon how to bill insurance and I found that *all* of the financial files were missing. The year was off to a rough start, but at least I had a trustworthy and capable new friend by my side.

CHAPTER 25

Hug My Doctor

I LUCKED OUT IN HIRING Sharon. True to her word, she was perfectly capable of running the office herself. The two of us had a good time working together; we just seemed to click and understand one another. Her work ethic and intelligence helped a lot too. But I also appreciated her sense of humor. I recently came across an old note she wrote me:

Dear Joey:

In the event that I should ever displease you with my duties, I am writing the list of qualifications that you could place in the newspaper for my replacement.... (Before you get all hyper, I did this at home and not on your time) AND, IT'S JUST FOR FUN!!!

WANTED

Do you want a challenge? Are you healthy? Do you like the smell of Lysol? Can you run fast? I've got a job for you... This is really a luxury position, plush air-conditioned office, it's 45 degrees due to the employer/Doctor being a hot-blooded Italian swinger. If you can meet the qualifications listed below, boy, have we been looking everywhere for you!

DUTIES

Can you keep a straight face when everybody thinks you and the Doctor are having an affair? Can you take EKG's without becoming unglued when a man removes his wooden leg so you can attach the leads?

Do you sing, dance, tell jokes or do bird calls to entertain patients when the Doctor is an hour overdue because he's checking out a new bod at the hospital (38-24-26)? Are you strong-willed, patient, and a little deaf? You'll work out just fine when our "golden oldies" call.

Can you speak a foreign language? Does it happen to be New Jersey-Italian? "Dictation...Dictation"

Are you prone to writer's cramp? Too bad sweetie, you have to keep ledgers, day sheets, daily, weekly, monthly and yearly totals of the income and out flow of the money. All insurances, keep charges up to date, file correspondence, lab reports, H&P's, payment receipts, make photocopies. Can you order supplies? Can you make bank deposits, do reconciliations, and keep the books straight?

Do you eat fast? You get an hour for lunch – and while you got all this "free time" you might stop at the Post Office and buy stamps and go to the bank and deposit all the money you've begged out of the patients, while you're enjoying your walk, why not stop off at the hospital and collect all the insurance data necessary for collecting more money.

Do you have a good memory...can you be kind and discreet when America's Sweetheart lines up two dates on the same day at the same time and he can't even remember their names? (I'll never forget what's-her-name).

How's your back? Hope it's good and strong because the Doctor gets an itch at least once a week to rearrange the furniture. (I do hope your legs don't cramp easily because you can be sure half the stuff will end up under your desk, baby.) After this little bit of work and your vitamin pills haven't worn off...are you any good at making beds, polishing furniture, filling paper towel holders, changing table paper, etc.?

Can you grit your teeth when the doctor asks you at the end of the day, "Is Everything done?"

I'd sign my name, but I'm too tired.

My mom would stop by the office occasionally and became fast friends with Sharon. However, she was very concerned about Sharon's weight, which would have been strange (given that Sharon was perfectly fit and healthy) if she weren't Italian. Like a stereotypical Italian mother, my mom took it upon herself to make sure everyone she cared about had plenty to eat. From that point on, she'd usually come to the office with a picnic basket full of Italian food. Then she'd start setting things up and say, "Eat, honey." Most of my girlfriends had to deal with the same situation anytime we visited my mother.

Sharon and I often brainstormed ways we could help teach practical medical skills to others. There were a lot of dentists in our building and it occurred to me that there was a high likelihood that at some point, someone would have a heart attack in the dentist's chair, especially since many people are afraid to be there. So Sharon and I set up a CPR class and encouraged everyone in the building to attend.

We had one of those dummies to demonstrate CPR and had many participants partake in a simulation. Some time later, while I was in the hospital, someone did in fact have a heart attack in the dentist's chair. This was before you could dial 911 (at least in California), so you had to dial "O" for operator, then they would connect you to the ambulance service. When the person had a heart attack, the dentist started doing CPR and his assistant called for me, but I was at the hospital. So Sharon ran up and helped him out. Fortunately, they were able to keep the guy alive until the ambulance arrived, then they took him to the hospital and he survived. I was shocked to hear that story when I came in to close up that day. Not because there was a heart attack – I dealt with patients suffering from cardiac arrest all the time – but because of the way the patient was saved in what seemed to be the nick of time.

It takes many types to keep a hospital running. Of course there are the doctors, the nurses, the administrative staff – but there are also many people behind the scenes, doing important work that is unfortunately largely unrecognized. One man I truly admired at St. Joseph's was Manuel, who was one of our janitors. Manuel was a first-generation immigrant from El Salvador whose joyful spirit lit up a room. He was always friendly and incredibly hardworking.

For years, I saw Manuel in passing and we would exchange the typical, "Good morning! How are you?" and a cordial reply. It never really extended farther than that until one day, while doing paperwork in my office, there was a hurried knock at my door.

"Come in," I said without looking up. Sharon burst in, looking drained.

"Manuel had a heart attack. Can you see him?"

"Yes, where is he?" I asked as I quickly rose and followed Sharon out the door. I was often called for these kinds of cases. My office was across the way from the hospital and I had a penchant for working on unexpected emergency cases.

Manuel was in a hospital bed, which was strange to see. I had only ever seen him hard at work; now he looked nearly lifeless. He was pale and rather limp. As I looked at him, one of the nurses, Mary, came over to debrief me.

"Apparently he was working as usual and around 3 pm, he had a heart attack. Fell to the floor. Thank God one of the nurses saw it happen and an EMT came right away."

"Wow. I guess if you're going to have a heart attack, the hospital is the place to do it," I said as I jotted down some notes. We discussed the case a little more and I went in to see Manuel.

"Manuel! How are you holding up?" I asked as I put my hand on his shoulder. His eyes were tired and he looked weary, far from his usual energetic self.

"Doctor…thank you for coming," he muttered. "I'm afraid. Didn't know I had heart problems."

"Many people don't," I replied. "Heart problems develop slowly, over time. When was the last time you had a checkup?"

"Not sure…" he said, trailing off. We discussed what had happened and I told him how he would be monitored for a while until he was stabilized. I took a look at the results and readings. His heart attack was severe and I knew right away that it would lead him to an early grave.

As soon as I would permit him to, Manuel was back at work, as cheerful as ever despite his pain. The warmth and positivity Manuel exuded never ceased to amaze me. One time I asked him where he got his great attitude. "I don't know, Doctor. I'm just so grateful for all I have in life: my family, my faith, my job…and that I'm still alive," he replied with a big smile as he continued mopping the floor.

Manuel continued to see me for a couple of years and I kept a close eye on his readings. I remained cautiously optimistic about his case, explaining that the heart attack took quite a toll, but that certain lifestyle changes could prolong his life expectancy.

Manuel was willing to make changes in his diet and life, so I did the best I could to make exercise and dietary suggestions that would likely lengthen his life. However, so much of his heart was destroyed in the heart attack that he didn't have sufficient strength to support his body for very long. When things got very bad, he finally left work and went home. With a heavy heart, I told him he should get his affairs in order and spend time with his family.

As the next two weeks went by, I would check on Manuel by phone. There was really nothing else I could do; he was dying, but I appreciated this warm, kind man and wanted him to know that I cared.

About two weeks after Manuel had left, Sharon transferred a call to my office. "Joe…it's Manuel's daughter, Marlene."

"Oh…oh boy, ok please transfer the call," I said, knowing what she was about to tell me.

"Dr. Turcillo?" Marlene said, as she cried on the phone.

"Yes, Marlene, it's me."

"He's gone," she paused and continued crying. "You can come over anytime now."

I knew that she wanted me to come by to pronounce him dead. This was one of the worst parts of my job, but of course I wanted to be there for Manuel's family. "Yes, I'll be there shortly," I replied.

When I arrived at their house, Marlene led me into a bedroom where I saw Manuel's lifeless body. His wife sat beside him, crying hard and muttering prayers in Spanish. I noticed a cross above the headboard on his bed. I paid my respects to Marlene and her mother. Looking at Manuel's wife, I said, "May I?" gesturing to Manuel. She nodded and held his hand.

I checked Manuel's pulse, as we have to do in order to pronounce someone dead. There was, of course, no heartbeat – just his cold skin. Of course, I had already known he was dead the second I saw him, and his family knew that too; this was just a matter of following protocol.

"Like you said, he is gone," I said solemnly. "I'm so sorry." I stood to leave, not wanting to invade their space. Suddenly, Manuel's daughter and wife got up and gave me a hug and a kiss. Surprised, I asked why they hugged me. After all, I hadn't been able to save Manuel.

"A few hours ago, my father said, 'Once my doctor pronounces me dead, you should get up and give him a hug and a kiss,'" Marlene said through her tears. "He knew you did everything you could to help him. We thank you very much."

I gently held her hands and nodded to her. "Your father was a wonderful man," I said before heading back to the hospital. I was touched to know Manuel appreciated me so much and will always remember his joyful spirit.

CHAPTER 26

The Divorced Dads' Club

———

ALL MY LIFE, I'VE HABITUALLY collected things, much to the chagrin of my girlfriends, wife, and children. I must have learned this tendency from my mother, who salvaged anything and everything. I always gave her money and anything she needed, but sometimes I disliked giving her cash because she would stash it in the strangest places. I once opened the oven and found $1,500 cash sitting inside. I had to commend her, though, for that hiding place. It was probably the first and only time I opened the oven in that house. I ultimately figured I couldn't change her ways; it had been a habit for so long.

Pat, who lives very minimally, and my daughter have accused me of hoarding, but I consider it a careful collection of items that are either useful or have sentimental value. Once I started studying medicine, even when I was a teen, I would keep a first aid kit. At first it had the cheapest supplies, given what I could afford. That kit grew and grew as I learned exponentially more about medicine and the vast array of things that can go wrong in the human body. By the time I was a parent, I could practically help people with anything but surgery from all the medical supplies I had curated over the years. I needed a place to store it all and while the garage sufficed, I wanted something more mobile.

The next logical step was to get a camper van. This way, I could use it to camp with the kids and friends and when it wasn't in use, I could store all my medical supplies in it. In the event of some sort of disaster, I could easily evacuate with everything we'd need to survive. When Pat saw the camper for the first time, before I took the kids out for a trip, she joked that I was prepared for whatever: a fire, a flood, a tsunami.

Of course, the medical supplies continued to grow and eventually I couldn't contain them in my small camper. So now I have them in my garage and in the house as well. Nancy in particular would get worked up about the glut of possessions. As a nurse and stewardess, she was very organized and used to living a lean and nimble lifestyle. Coming to my house and seeing my vast collections of books, pictures, and medical supplies piled around stressed her out. In defense, I'd explain that many of my items were useful.

"Nancy, if there's a huge earthquake or fire you'll be thankful that I have everything we'd need to survive," I'd say.

"If there was a disaster, you wouldn't be able to *find* anything in this place because it's such a mess," she retorted. "Or something would topple over and hit someone on the head, so at the end of the day, you're no better off than anyone else." That made me pause for a moment. She definitely had a point; in a big earthquake, many things would topple over...and it would be difficult to efficiently find certain supplies. I suppose having them just makes me feel better. It also gives me satisfaction knowing that I could help out my family and neighbors. Many of my friends joke that if there's a disaster, they're coming over to my house.

Most people tend to give me a pass on the survival material, but I've never been able to get away with the amount of photos and books I like to keep around. My family has a point: My house is in a never-ending de-cluttering process, because I accumulate things far faster than I get rid of them. But I simply don't like throwing things away. For some reason, being surrounded by so many of my things gives me comfort, the same way my mother found it soothing. Likewise, I feel at home in my worn clothes. While I have plenty of nice outfits for my formal affairs, I'm most comfortable in my scrubs, white coat, or sweats.

The camper van itself is something I tried to sell for a while. But it was hard to part with. Storing all my supplies in the garage wouldn't be the same as having them mobile. Then there are also the fond memories I have of spending time with the kids on camping trips. We would go camping with a group Lisa dubbed "The Dads who are Divorced Club," which was mostly a group of other divorced doctors and their children.

As kids, Lisa and Susie always had a sense of adventure and were ecstatic when we'd start planning a camping trip. We'd get all the supplies ready and they would curiously examine the odds and ends I had stored in the camper. I'd explain the purpose of different contraptions to them. We rarely used any of these materials, which is fortunate.

Sometimes I recruited friends and coworkers to help me take care of the kids, because I enjoyed surrounding myself with a lot of people while I socialized. It was also reassuring to have the assistance of women who were used to taking care of kids. Sharon often spent time with the kids and me and grew very close to them. There was also a nurse named Imgard who became like family to us. Imgard was one of the most impressive people I've ever known. She was a German immigrant and knew more than any other nurse I worked with. In fact, she often knew more than some doctors. I often said that if I ever were hospitalized, I'd want Imgard to be my nurse. The way she cared for patients was above and beyond, so I always felt secure when she was looking after the kids with me.

Over time, Imgard and her husband, Fritz, became like family and we'd celebrate holidays with them. Imgard celebrated Christmas the old German way and invited my kids and me to join her family. The kids and I stared in wonder, and with a bit of worry, when we saw the lights on the tree were actual candles. We'd sing "*O Tannenbaum*," (the German version of "Oh Christmas Tree") as we gathered around the tree. Continuing the German tradition, we sometimes went to a German themed place called Manson Ranch, where the kids dressed in lederhosen and we all picnicked. In those moments, it felt almost as if I weren't a divorced parent, but that we were part of a larger family.

Lisa and Susie in lederhosen

Though I did make time for our family outings, I didn't make enough time; I was very preoccupied with work and dating. In between seeing Nancy (and while I was with her) I continued dating different women. One of the more memorable ones was Michelle. She was a big director's sister and lived in Bel Air. I had an open invitation to go anytime I wanted. No obligations, just the option to drop by her palatial home whenever convenient. She was happy anytime I stopped by and would cook for me and make me feel right at home. I'd lean back in a lounge chair by the pool and think to myself: I have captain's paradise. Michelle's family and I loved each other, too, but ultimately the relationship wasn't compelling enough to take to the next level.

I also started seeing an actor's wife once they were in the divorce process. Her name was Abigail and she hustled me for months before I relented. I couldn't allow myself to see her while she was still married – there is an Italian code that you can never sleep with another man's wife – but once they were separated, I figured I had the green light. I first met her at work, when her parents came in for a complicated case. She wasn't my patient, but I saw her often while I was treating her parents. And once we started dating, all this girl wanted me to do was make love to her. All the time. When we went out, she picked up the tab. I shared that with a buddy of mine and he looked at me quizzically.

"You don't mind the woman paying?" he asked.

"Me? No. I figure if they wanna take care of me – please, go right ahead. I need help," I replied with a chuckle.

Another girl I dated around that time was a pilot named Sherry. I loved hearing her stories about flying, although I declined to join her for a ride. Flying had always fascinated me, but I hated partaking in the activity. Sherry was a pro, though, and trained others to become pilots. Susie really liked her because of their shared enthusiasm for aviation.

Of all my girlfriends, Nancy spent the most time with the kids. She was actually the only girlfriend I ever had that they both really liked. I'm not sure how much Nancy caught on when I was dating other women. People tipped her off, but like my wife, she seemed to look the other way. Though our relationship spanned ten years, it was on and off at times. We'd get into an argument and go our separate ways, but something always seemed to bring us back together. After our biggest fight, we both assumed it was truly over. But then a couple of years later, I was walking down Rodeo Drive and, to my complete surprise, saw Nancy. We started talking and then got a cup of coffee and the next thing I knew, we were dating again. That also didn't last, though, and eventually we stopped talking for good, it seemed.

CHAPTER 27

On The Up and Up

"JOE, YOU BETTER FORGET IT, she's gonna die," my colleague, Dr. Brian, said solemnly. He was what you would consider an office doctor, the type that could treat a cold and assist in surgery. They often called on me to assess situations because I was an internist and studied the inner workings of the body. I had a talent for seeing the big picture and making connections other doctors, who specialized in specific areas, often missed. Dr. Brian had called asking for me to assess a woman whose body was responding adversely to the treatment her heart seemed to require, but just minutes later he called back and rescinded his request.

"I'll be right there," I replied. I hung up before he had a chance to change his mind.

Running upstairs to the ICU, I opened the door and, out of breath, observed a shell of a person hunched over as if she were some kind of animal. I knew she was a woman from Dr. Brian's phone call, but if I hadn't been told her sex, it may have taken me a few seconds to determine that, because she looked so hollow and lifeless. It was the early morning and after a busy night at the hospital, all I could think was: What the hell is going on?

We knew Mrs. Miller had mitral stenosis (which is when the mitral valve in the heart is restricted, causing decreased blood flow), which the doctors were treating her for. The nurse made adjustments to the IV as I was flooded with charts. This fifty-year-old woman had been in and out of the hospital like a yo-yo for years due to her low blood pressure and heart disease.

Her husband sat nervously in the corner, wringing his hands. "She's not responding too well," he said, then looked down.

I nodded in agreement and said, "I'm here to try and change that." As I went through the charts, there was one study that stood out, a thyroid study. She had a low thyroid. This was my one lead, so I requested further tests to narrow down some possibilities.

One thing that tipped me off was that Mrs. Miller didn't look very much like a woman. Well, she looked more like a woman than a man, but let's just say you wouldn't want to be married to her. After confirming that her appearance had dramatically changed, I wondered what her hormone levels were and requested tests for that.

The hormone tests led me to the conclusion that Mrs. Miller had hypopituitarism, which is when the pituitary gland (which you can consider the "master gland" of the brain) isn't producing enough hormones. When most of the hormones are being under-produced, a person has panhypopituitarism ("pan" meaning all).

Hypopituitarism can occur many ways. One reason it could occur is that some women can hemorrhage into the pituitary gland while giving birth. The pituitary gland produces several hormones such as thyroid-stimulating hormones (TSH). The master gland also tells the thyroid if it's not producing enough. Or it may tell the adrenal cortex, "Hey, produce some more adrenocorticotropic hormones (ACTH)."

Here's the kicker. We all knew she had mitral stenosis but the two heart specialists she had weren't picking up on any hormonal problems that indicated hypopituitarism. The cardiologists knew that the mitral valve separates the left ventricle chamber from the right ventricle chamber and that she had heart catheterization. These doctors were in the left ventricle, so to speak; all they saw was the left ventricle, they weren't looking at the whole body. As they say in today's vogue, they weren't "holistic."[2]

---

2 I hate the distinction some doctors give themselves as being "holistic." I run away from a doctor that advertises he's holistic. All doctors are – or at least should be – holistic. If you're a great doctor, you're automatically holistic.

Because this woman had mitral valve heart disease, other doctors had put her on a low salt diet, which happens to be one of the worst things you could do to a woman with hypopituitarism. When the pituitary gland is not functioning, it's preventing other hormones from retaining enough sodium. Sodium retention is maintained by different mechanisms in our bodies. It boosts blood volume. Yet all of the doctors she saw, being cardiologists, insisted on putting her on a low salt diet.

That's why she came into the hospital with hypotension. Without salt, she had no blood volume, so her blood pressure went dangerously low. Immediately after I shared my findings and the cardiologists stopped thinking solely in terms of her heart disease, we gave her salt and salt retaining medicines. Suddenly, she started changing – she seemed to slowly start coming "back to life."

I also prescribed her sex hormones because her sex organs were deprived of estrogen. A few weeks later, Mrs. Miller's husband turned to me and said, "I can't believe it. I have a wife again. She's becoming a woman again." Of course she was "becoming a woman" again, I thought. She had been deprived of all of the hormones that gave her femininity. Once the hypopituitarism was properly addressed, she walked out of the hospital looking and feeling fine. Sure, like many patients, she had heart disease, but that actually wasn't the problem in this instance. For whatever reason, she had suffered a pituitary stroke, if you will. But once her hormones were balanced again and her diet was changed, she walked out of the hospital and returned home.

A few weeks after seeing Mrs. Miller, I got a message from a colleague of mine informing me that I was elected President of the Verdugo Division of the American Heart Association, which was an unexpected but welcomed honor. To celebrate, there was a fund raising party for the organization where the former president announced that I was the new president.

I excitedly relayed the news to my new girlfriend, who also happened to be named Pat, on our date that night. I had started dating this Pat shortly after the divorce, but it had mostly been in secret, because her old fashioned Italian parents weren't pleased that she was dating a man who was divorced with two kids.

However, they did appreciate my career as a doctor and I suppose that's the only reason they tolerated me. But it quickly became known that our relationship was not going to be approved of, which was a big predicament for Pat. Nevertheless, she was also in love with me, so we ended up dating in secret for a year. I don't know what it was about Pat, but something made me think I could change my ways for her. What exactly, I couldn't put my finger on. Of course she was beautiful, kind, and smart. She worked as a teacher, which I admired. As time went by, my affection toward her grew stronger and I started thinking about how we could make things work long-term.

I brought Pat to the Verdugo fundraiser as my date. All sorts of people were there, from my colleagues to a few celebrities. Lynda Carter, who was becoming very famous for her role in "Wonder Woman," was there to hand out awards. My mom and Sharon were there too. In fact, Sharon was the one who organized the whole evening.

One of the guests of honor was Mrs. Miller. I took great pride in introducing her and discussing her case and unexpected recovery. It was surreal to see her walking around at a gala, given how sick she'd been in the hospital. After discussing her case, I sat down and the former president got up and introduced me as the new president of our division.

When he called me to the stage, my mom jumped up and yelled, "Joey! That's my Joey" among the applause. I smiled at her enthusiasm and considered how special it must be for her to go to such an event. If it weren't for me, she never would have come to California or seen anything like parties of that magnitude.

After the ceremony was over, I spoke with Lynda Carter and, like the rest of America, was instantly enamored. We seemed to get along well so I asked her to lunch and was equally surprised and delighted when she said yes.

At the gala with guests, including Lynda Carter (top, second from left)

CHAPTER 28

Wonder Woman

———

OVER A NICE LUNCH IN Beverly Hills, Lynda and I spoke of all sorts of things, including our families. I told her how much my daughter Lisa loved watching "Wonder Woman" and about the "Charlie's Angels" magazine clippings in her scrapbook. Lynda smiled and graciously suggested I bring the kids to the set sometime. I was surprised for a moment and didn't say anything, then eagerly accepted.

"I can't wait to see the look on the girls' faces when I tell them they're going to meet Wonder Woman," I joyously admitted. The girls were eight and ten at the time. Getting to miss class to meet one of the most famous women in the world on set would be a dream come true.

A few days later, I surprised the kids at school. First I pulled Susie out of class and told her what we were doing. Susie's biggest interests were trucks, planes, and cars, but she also frequently watched Lynda Carter's shows with her big sister. In any event, she was thrilled to spend a few hours out of class.

Lisa, on the other hand, was ecstatic. When I picked her up at lunchtime and told her what we were doing, her jaw dropped. Some of her friends were sitting beside her and looks of shock and envy flashed across their faces.

"We're going to see Wonder Woman?" Lisa squealed.

"Yes! Let's go! Filming starts soon," I said excitedly. Lisa quickly said goodbye to her friends and ran off to join Susie and me. We cruised over to the set in the Porsche, singing along to some of our favorite tunes.

Once we arrived on set, all three of us were wide-eyed as we got a behind the scenes look at the show. The kids were fascinated by the imaginary world that was being staged and all the people rushing around doing their respective jobs. A young woman who took our passes got an intern to give us a tour. She pointed out various elements and we all followed her gazing around.

"And that," the guide announced enthusiastically toward the end of our tour, "is Wonder Woman's invisible plane!" I laughed at her joke but Lisa and Susie looked around confusedly.

"Where?" Lisa asked.

The tour guide pointed off into the distance. "Well, see all the props around it? You can't actually see the plane, because it's *invisible.*"

"Oh," Lisa smiled, knowing she was in on the secret. Susie looked disappointed. She hoped to see a real plane.

As our tour wrapped up, someone tapped me on the shoulder and I turned around to see Lynda in full costume.

"Hello!" I greeted her. "Kids, look, Wonder Woman is here!" Lisa and Susie looked up in wonder, clearly star struck. This was their first time meeting someone famous.

Lynda greeted us all warmly and showed us a few details of the set. Then she asked an assistant for some photos and he brought over pictures for her to sign for the kids. Lisa and Susie smiled as she handed them her autographed eight-by-ten glossy portraits. Shortly afterwards, she had to get back to set and we watched some of the filming together for a while.

By the time I brought the kids back to campus, the school day was almost over. The kids gave me a big hug and a kiss before running excitedly back to class. I smiled as I imagined them showing their friends Lynda's autographed portrait and talking about their experience on set. Delighting my children provided a deep joy that couldn't be replicated by anything else.

Looking back on it, I wasn't that disappointed when things didn't pan out with Lynda, because I was more interested in Pat. The only problem was that I hadn't seen her since the night of the fundraiser. I began to wonder why she wasn't contacting me as she usually did. After a number of relationships and countless dates, I formed an opinion that a good relationship depended on the woman chasing after the man and that I needed a woman who would fight for me. Once it seemed Pat didn't want to fight for me, I started to back off.

CHAPTER 29

Superego

―――――――――

AFTER PARTING WAYS WITH THE second Pat, I had to wonder if I was ever going to find the kind of love that I was looking for: the sort of love that supposedly makes one feel complete. Right around the time I stopped seeing her, I had a dream that I couldn't shake. I woke up one morning remembering I dreamt I was holding hands with someone in a serene, ethereal place and I thought the hand was my father's. The dream seemed to take place in the heavens, as I was surrounded by a cloud-like atmosphere. I felt completely safe. But then all of a sudden, I felt disconnected and looked down at my hand and saw I was holding hands with no one; I was alone.

I wanted to better understand myself and know what my dream meant. Perhaps more importantly, I wanted to understand why I had so many unresolved relationships with women. Desperately wanting to figure out why I couldn't settle down with one woman or find the right woman, I booked an appointment with a therapist.

Confession was the closest thing to therapy that I'd ever done. Now I sat before a Jewish therapist, a kind older gentleman named Dan, who I could see clearly, unlike the priests I used to sit beside in the confession booth. Given that it was my first time in therapy, I didn't really know what to do, so I started spilling out everything I thought he should know: my childhood, all the things I'd done wrong, my goal to find the perfect woman.

"Slow down, Joe," Dan said gently, with a warm smile. "Let's just take this one piece at a time." I realized that I was acting like I was in confession, sharing my sins one by one. So I dialed it back and went into more detail about my childhood. Then I started telling him about the dream.

Dan's analysis of the dream was that, beyond wanting more of a connection with my father, I had some kind of a yearning for God. I'm sure a lot of people feel that way, like they need God or something larger to believe in. We all wonder why, if God is real, there is such evil in the world. Looking back, I see that I was still innocent in a way. Even after all the deaths I'd seen and all the girls I'd fooled around with, I was still a child at heart.

By the next session, I started telling Dan about my divorce and all the girls I'd dated since then, expressing my concern that I wasn't finding the right woman to settle down with. He said something to the effect of, "Seems like you're happy dating a lot of women. Do you want to settle down?"

And I had to pause and think. "Well, somewhere along the line I just can't be single all the while. I mean I could have married many other girls...but I gotta have a special girl to me. I need what's difficult to get. I always say this tongue-in-cheek; I say it with some temerity and some truthfulness – I need a girl that's got a 'Radcliffe' mind and a 'Chorus Line' body." Dan was silent. "Now I really don't mean that, but it ain't too far from the truth," I added.

Dan raised his eyebrows a bit, saying, "I see."

"Hey, I'm no angel," I said, echoing one of my father's favorite phrases. "Don't misunderstand me. I grew up, I've been no angel...I've been selfish. But I still have that little boy inside of me. Never forgot it."

"The little boy who was upset by injustice? Is that what you mean?" he asked, referring to the story I told him about the little dog – the story my mom made up that had such an impact on me as a child.

"Yeah, well, not just that... Let me show you something, Doc," I said. "I have to show you this. If I don't, I'm afraid you won't be able to understand me." I pulled my wallet out from my back pocket and fumbled through it until I found the picture I was searching for: the portrait taken when I was four, where I look frightened. I leaned forward and handed it to him, adding, "That picture can probably say more about it than I can."

He examined it for a moment.

"Look closely. Look at the eyes," I suggested.

After some consideration, the kind of pointedly long pause that therapists take, he said, "The boy looks very sad and scared."

"Scared – you hit the nail on the head. That's it."

"This is you, right?"

"That's me. Sometimes I feel like that's still who I really am. At least it's always been a part of me."

Another long pause. Then finally, Dan said, "Can you elaborate on that?"

"I've just always felt on my own, sometimes even when I'm surrounded by people I love. I guess that's part of the reason I'm here. It must be part of the reason why I have all these unresolved relationships."

Dan looked at me, nodded as if to show his attentiveness, then glanced back at the picture. "You know, Joe, I don't just see fear. I also see strength, a determination to push forward."

I fell silent, interested in his take. Dan was incredibly wise and smart and I hung on every word of his analysis. I hadn't really seen the picture that way. I'd always seen it as the struggling part of myself.

Dan and I discussed many things, but mainly focused on my relationship trouble. In trying to make sense of my relationships with women, Dan offered his opinion that I had a very strong superego.

"The superego is the part of us that is concerned with morals, right and wrong," he shared. Dan explained that I was extremely idealistic, and that when it came to romance, that idealism could be a problem, because it tended to create unreasonable expectations. As we examined things further, he pointed out that what I learned from Church and the copious amount of movies I saw as a young usher were probably big contributors to the idealism.

Dan pointed out that this wasn't a bad thing; it was good to have strong morals and high standards. But, he reiterated, it could pose problems when it came to relationships. My fantasy of having the 100% angel and the 100% beauty queen couldn't be met.

I saw Dan for a while. Another issue he helped handle pertained to a predicament at my hospital. By that time, I was Chief of Staff and had discovered that a couple of our surgeons had a tendency to send some patients into surgery when they shouldn't have. As a result, an inordinate amount of their patients had complications or even died due to their surgeries. Of course, there is always a huge risk to surgery. As they say, there is no such thing as minor surgery, only minor surgeons. But if you know someone is a minor surgeon, you can't just look the other way – especially if it's happening on your watch. I knew I had to find a way to get these surgeons reviewed and taken out of my hospital. One was completely incompetent and the other was smart as a whiz, but took on tasks he wasn't qualified for.

It wasn't simple to fire them, though. They had reputations as big shot surgeons, probably because they graduated from some of the top medical schools. It reminded me of what Father Luyet often said, that good students can go to bad schools and bad students can go to good schools. I for one was certainly surprised to discover that graduates of such prestigious schools were shoddy surgeons.

To complicate matters further, one of these surgeons was a good friend of mine. Firing someone is always an awful feeling and it gets exponentially worse the more you know the person. But I had to protect patients above all else, so I reported them. Not long after, the one who was formerly a good friend sued the hospital and I had to go to depositions and get dragged through some of that legal mud. But ultimately, my convictions were confirmed: They were ousted on the grounds that they were unfit to work as surgeons. When I told Dan about how conflicted I felt by the whole situation, he looked at me kindly and said something unexpected. I'd learned to not expect him to say anything, as most of the time he was silent.

"Don't try to be Jesus Christ. You know what they did to him."

I laughed at his joke but took part of the message to heart. I was doing my best and in this situation, there was no easy way out. Doing the right thing was painful but I knew I was watching out for the patients, which was my main priority.

CHAPTER 30

Chorus Line

———

NOBODY THREW A PARTY LIKE the Lombardis, patients of mine who I grew close to over the years. Their Halloween and New Year's Eve parties were like nothing I'd seen before. It seemed like everyone was there – even people who weren't invited. Max, their son, often told me he didn't recognize many of the attendees. But his parents welcomed them in anyway. After a couple of drinks, I'd often get on stage and sing Sinatra with the band, which Max – a classically trained instrumentalist – got a kick out of. I was always impressed by the people they would have come and perform, like Bill Farrell and Whoopi Goldberg. After decades of throwing these parties, the Lombardis eventually stopped in their old age, but for years, people would still show up at the door expecting another party.

One night Max and I were going to a few of our usual spots. At this time period, I usually would give my business card to women in order to have them call me. The night was going well and we had met some nice women when I went up to a beautiful girl and started talking to her. She seemed a bit guarded. After telling her my name and exchanging a few words, I went to pull out my card and she looked at me and said, "Oh I don't need your card. I know who you are. You're Dr. Turcillo from St. Joseph's. You went out with my girlfriend Sandy and my girlfriend Reina and my girlfriend Samantha. I don't need your card."

I was a bit stumped there. Max had seen the whole thing but held his tongue. As we walked away, he laughed and said, "Well, I think this place is used up for you, Joe. On to the next bar."

And of course there were always more bars and more women. Our other buddy, Richmond, would also cruise around town with us. I loved talking to Richmond because he was a director and it was fascinating to hear about his projects, which were usually plays.

Max and I got into the habit of going to Marina Del Rey once a week after work. Richmond joined us when he could, but usually had to work late. There were a few bars with live music that Max was particularly fond of. Usually it was the same routine, except one time when I got a call right before I was planning to head out.

"Joe, I'm not feeling very well," a strained voice said. I could hear the suffering right away; my typically upbeat, cheerful friend was clearly struggling.

"You alright?" I asked him.

"I'm not in any pain. I'm just incredibly tired," he explained. "On my run this morning I got tired so quickly."

"What are your symptoms?" I asked.

"Haven't been feeling good. I just went to my doctor and he said it looks like I'm coming down with the flu. He said to call him if it didn't get better in a few days."

I proceeded to ask him many questions, suspecting that it was something more severe than the flu. "I'll need to see you in person to get a complete examination," I told him.

Once I got over to Max's, I began checking his vitals. Everything seemed alright, so I proceeded to do some additional tests. Nothing was checking out so eventually, I told him I had to do a rectal exam. Nobody wants to have a rectal exam done (and no one wants to administer them, either), but it's a standard practice to check for certain problems. So I put my gloves on and started the test.

Just as I asked if he felt any pain, he let out a small yelp and said, "Yes, that hurts! Badly." Then I suspected he had appendicitis. I insisted he see one of my surgeon friends to check.

"It's almost six o'clock, Joe. Offices are closed."

"Let me make a few calls," I said. I called a surgeon friend of mine, Danny, and explained the situation.

"Bring him in right away," Danny replied and hung up.

Fifteen minutes later we were in Danny's office. He examined Max in about two minutes.

"You'll be in emergency surgery within thirty minutes. A nurse will be in shortly to prep you," Danny said coolly. He didn't have the best bedside manner but he was a great surgeon. Max, of course, was shocked.

"What?" he almost yelled. "But I'm not in any pain."

"Your appendix is going to burst. We have to take it out before that happens." That silenced Max.

After his surgery, it turned out he already had gangrene throughout his intestines and he was told he would have been dead if he hadn't had the emergency surgery.

"Boy, it's a good thing we didn't go out tonight," Max said when I visited him in recovery.

After the appendix incident, Max trusted me completely. He and his family sought my advice on all sorts of medical matters, but most of our time together was social. Max and his family introduced me to many people over the years. Some of the most memorable were their German friends, a couple who was visiting Los Angeles for the first time. I told them about my friends Fritz and Imgard and suggested they come to dinner with us all sometime. They were thrilled and asked us for recommendations around the city. As we started sharing our favorite spots, I suggested I show them around. Nothing like seeing a city with a local.

As it turned out, I happened in to some tickets to the Los Angeles debut of *A Chorus Line*, the hit Broadway musical. I was thrilled to see it, as I'd always loved musicals and going to the premiere would be a flashy, star-studded event. I invited the German couple to join me, realizing this would truly be a once-in-a-lifetime experience for them.

After they returned to Germany, full of stories about their experiences in Los Angeles, they sent me a thank you note along with a wooden sign that said, "Joe, Actor of Life." I held the sign and wondered what they meant by that. Based on the profuse gratitude expressed in the accompanying note, I took it as a compliment and hung the sign up in my den. Sometimes I look at it and wonder what it really means and if I am, in fact, an actor of life.

CHAPTER 31

Grandpa Joe

———

THE DAY LISA TURNED SIXTEEN, I showed up unannounced and wished her a happy birthday.

After a few minutes of catching up, I said, "Get your things. We're going to get your license."

"What?" Lisa asked, surprised.

"You're sixteen! Let's go get your license." I was excited for her to experience the freedom of having her own car to drive around.

"Dad…I don't think I'm ready yet," she said shyly.

"That's nonsense. Of course you're ready – you're a Turcillo." And with that, we were off to the DMV.

As I expected, Lisa passed her test. Years later, she mentioned that when I said, "Of course you're ready – you're a Turcillo," it gave her a bit of extra confidence to believe she could pass her test, even though she didn't feel sufficiently prepared.

Susie was ready to get her license the day she turned sixteen, probably because she had seen Lisa driving for a couple of years and was eager to get behind the wheel herself. And because I had taught the kids to drive long before they were sixteen. I used to let them turn the wheel on my lap while we drove down empty streets. Seeing her legally behind the wheel for the first time reminded me of when I was driving my aunt around in her fancy cars – she was in her glory. Susie knew how to enjoy her free time and was an excellent athlete, but her dyslexia posed an enormous challenge to her in school and for future work prospects.

Many people still didn't know what dyslexia was or how to diagnose it and even when they did, the treatments simply weren't very effective. And by the time we really found out what Susie's disability was, she had already fallen so far behind her classmates. For years she was bullied about her academic performance, and it slowly ate away at her confidence. As a little kid, she had been full of light and energy, but as the years wore on, she became very depressed. Although many kids made fun of her, her teammates and a group of black girls befriended her and stood up for her, eventually kind of protecting her from the insults of the other students. I've always been incredibly thankful to those women for helping Susie. One of them, Monique, still calls me up every now and then and says, "How's it going, Doc?" It always brightens my day to hear from her.

Although classroom activities were a huge struggle for Susie, she excelled in sports. So did Lisa. Both kids were quite athletic, playing soccer and other sports. Susie played as many sports as she could: soccer, softball, and basketball. She was able to shine on the fields and the court, often winning athletic awards. Lisa was a cheerleader and a soccer player. I didn't really go to their games, because they were usually when I was in the office or hospital. I also wasn't very interested in sports.

I did enjoy other sorts of activities with them, though. As a tomboy, Susie would happily partake in outings like shooting or off-roading or checking out new cars. Lisa was more feminine, so sometimes I would take her to charity or work events. It was always great to have Lisa there and introduce her to my colleagues. Susie wasn't interested in those affairs; she had no desire to dress up and be fancy.

Out of the blue, I got a call from my father, who was living in Trinidad and working as a mason. Hearing his voice on the line was almost like hearing a ghost from the past, given how little I ever heard from him.

"Joe," he croaked, sounding weak, "I'm very ill. The hospitals here are shit. I gotta get to America."

That was all he had to say. I booked a flight for him that day. I didn't want him in some hospital in the Caribbean. The only doctor I could fully trust to look after him was myself. The staff at St. Joseph Hospital sure got a kick out of him, this rough Italian-American from Jersey with a fearless attitude and a huge tattoo of a topless mermaid on his forearm.

One day I walked in his hospital room and was shocked to find him getting Holy Communion. I stared in confusion. It was the first time I'd ever seen or heard of my dad doing anything spiritual.

"Hey Dad, when did you get religious?" I asked.

He turned to me and asked, "'Ey, what do you take me for? An animal?"

Once my dad was stabilized, I was excited to introduce him to my kids. I hadn't talked to him about them much, because we hardly ever wrote each other and, at least from my experience growing up, I gathered that my dad wouldn't be that interested. Nevertheless, I was eager to introduce them. I called my kids and told them to meet me at the hospital the next day so that they could meet their grandfather. They seemed a bit pleased and a bit confused, understandably – they knew very little about Joe Sr. and may have heard some questionable things about him over the years.

Walking in to the hospital room the next day, with one of my kids on each side, I beamed at my dad. My girls had big hearts and were beautiful; I was always proud to introduce them to people, but this was special: I was introducing them to my father. He cranked his head up a little bit and looked at us with a mixture of confusion and indifference.

"Who the hell are they?" he asked in his rough Jersey accent. I was at a loss for words for a second, caught between reactions of concern and laughter. Humor won out and I let out a small laugh.

"Dad, these are your grandkids," I said through the laughter. "This is Lisa and this is Susie." I turned to them, unsure what to say. They both looked up at me with straight faces, clearly confused by the situation at hand. "Girls," I said with a slightly apologetic look, "this is your Grandpa Joe." They gazed back at him and maybe muttered a quiet, "Hello."

After getting discharged from the hospital, my dad was able to interact with my kids more. I took him to my house and showed him around town a bit. I'd have to ask him to watch his language, as he wasn't used to censoring himself in Trinidad. Or probably any other place he'd ever been, for that matter. As he started to get better, I sat down with him to talk.

"Hey, Dad, you know your health isn't very good. Why don't you stay here? I can look after you that way," I offered. I was enjoying seeing him and caring for him, but more importantly, I was confident the healthcare in Trinidad was dismal, at least in comparison to LA.

"No, Joey, I got to get back to the island and my business," he said. And there was no persuading him otherwise.

A few months later, I got another call from my dad. He was sick again and wanted to return to LA. Without hesitation, I bought him a plane ticket and drove him to the hospital when he arrived. As the years went by, he flew back and forth a few times for medical care.

One year, after healing up a bit, he realized the yard around my home could use a brick wall to hold back some of the plants that were overgrowing on a walkway. So he started laying bricks. Susie was curious about what he was doing and he started teaching her to lay bricks. I was surprised when I came home and saw Susie laying bricks herself, as if it were her job, as my father looked on. She learned how to lay the bricks within a day at the most and then proceeded to lay the bricks all around the house, even earning my father's approval, which wasn't given easily.

"Wow, I'm impressed you took the time to teach her that," I admitted.

Susie, my father, me, and my mother

"There's a lot of good in me, you know," he said with a sly smile. It was one of his favorite lines. And though it was said half jokingly, it always rang true.

Every time my dad returned to the hospital, it was entertaining for me to see how the hospital staff remembered him and loved him. They'd ask him how the Caribbean was and when he was going to move to Los Angeles for good. He'd scowl at them as if they were crazy and say, "Never."

When my dad left for Trinidad for the last time, I again asked if he would stay, considering his health. As always, he declined. That was the last time I saw him. His health failed shortly after his return. Although I was sad about his passing, it didn't change my daily life much, because I'd barely ever seen him since his arrest when I was a kid.

Losing him did make me reflect on where I was in my life, though. My career was in a good place and I had wonderful friends, but I still hadn't found the right mate. As I had many times before, I wondered whether or not true love really existed between romantic partners. And then, after years of doubt, my question was answered – right in my office.

When I saw one of my former colleagues being pushed into my office in a wheelchair by his gorgeous wife, I was surprised. I knew he retired a few years back, but I didn't know why he was in a wheelchair. It turned out he was incontinent and in diapers. I jotted down some notes on my notepad and paused, watching her tenderly taking care of her husband. I had never seen this kind of devotion with my own eyes. So, there really is love like that; it's not just in the movies, I thought to myself. Some patients you never forget. After they left, I asked myself if I would stick by my lady if I had to do that.

A while later, just the opposite happened. A man carried his wife in my office. I was confused as to why he was carrying her. He explained that she had Alzheimer's and was incontinent. This man was strong and fairly attractive, caring for his wife as tenderly as the actress I'd seen take care of her wheelchair-bound husband. When the first couple had come in, I thought maybe they were just an extreme anomaly, but after seeing this second couple, I felt I had seen the strength of romantic love. I couldn't deny love's place anymore. It was as if seeing those two couples allowed me to understand that when you love that deeply, it's adding a new soul to your own. And if you lost that person, you lost part of your own soul. As the man carried his wife out after their visit, I knew that a love that deep could endure anything. Perhaps not just love, but love and devotion. Love and devotion are complementary. Whether one can do without the other, I don't know, but the two together are dynamite.

CHAPTER 32

Healing A Heart

I GOT USED TO SEEING Mrs. Miller for routine checkups over the years, as she was still living with mitral stenosis. All was going well and I was pleased with her progress, until a few years after her first visit when I got another panicked call. The nurse told me Mrs. Miller's heart was failing and I rushed up to the ICU. Her life was even more precarious in this instance, as her heart was failing completely. It was the early morning again – these things always seemed to happen in the early morning when no one was around. It was only me and a small Filipino nurse tending to her when we realized her heart was stopping. There were no surgeons around and I didn't have time to think about calling anybody – I had to take care of it myself.

As an internist, this kind of treatment was not in my realm of care, but when you're the only doctor around, you have to do what you can. I had no time to consider what to do to save this woman's life – I had to make an immediate decision. I knew Mrs. Miller needed a temporary pacemaker that would trigger a heartbeat. As her heart had stopped beating on its own, I started hitting her chest every couple of seconds to force a beat.

I remembered my former teacher at LA County General Hospital, Dr. Izeri, an innovative cardiologist. Dr. Izeri invented a long needle that was used as a pacemaker needle. You could put the needle in directly and put a pacemaker wire through the needle. The pacemaker wire would cause a beat to occur without me having to hit her chest. I knew this was what I needed to do for Mrs. Miller, but I had never done it before and had never been properly trained to do so. I only knew how to do it theoretically.

With my left hand I continued to hit her chest and my right hand held the long needle that would allow me to place the temporary pacemaker. I thought hey, what the hell else has she got to go on? There wasn't time to think about it, so I took action. With the first shot – pure luck – I got the needle in the right side of the ventricle. As soon as I got it in, I put the pacemaker wire into the wall of the right ventricle. I waited for what felt like the longest few seconds of my life and then, wondrously, the heart started beating. I looked up at the nurse, who I hadn't noticed during the debacle, but I knew she had witnessed the entire process. After catching our breath, we shared a sigh of relief and smiled at each other and Mrs. Miller.

I was proud of myself for being the best I could have been under those circumstances. Maybe I could have done better with formal training, but when it came to these sorts of procedures, I was largely self-taught, you might say. In those days, I started the ICU at a hospital in Burbank and I taught nurses three days a week, three hours a day with a colleague. We taught internal medicine and intensive care, which I really enjoyed. Teaching also kept the material fresh in my head and required me to know it through and through. When it came to my patients, it didn't matter how much knowledge I had – I always ran scared, so even as I gained more and more experience, I studied more than ever. I was responsible for lives. I had to know this stuff cold.

Not long after reviving Mrs. Miller's heart, I got a letter from my old med school buddy, Gene Aronow. He updated me on his life and medical career and closed the letter by saying, "There's no one I know who wanted to be a doctor more than you and there's no one I know who would have made a better doctor than you." Some things I never forget, like those thoughtful words from a friend I always admired.

Part III

CHAPTER 33

Graduates

———

AFTER GRADUATING HIGH SCHOOL, LISA started modeling and traveled around quite a bit for work, even going to Japan. Susie stayed close by, eventually moving in to Pat's garage, which we converted into a loft for her. When Susie graduated, she was working and preparing to go to junior college and volunteering to help animals. Unfortunately, as she got older, she seemed to slip further into depression. As far as I could tell, her depression started when she was around thirteen or fourteen. She didn't tell me about it, but I could sense that she was sad and Pat and Lisa confirmed my suspicions. It broke my heart to see Susie depressed. I remembered one time, when we were visiting family in Jersey, she seemed particularly sad, apparently about a failed relationship. She was getting bored in Garfield and wanted to see her friends, so she asked if she could fly home early and I said that was fine. I tried to take advantage of any tangible opportunities to help lift her mood.

I didn't have experience in the mental health field but I wanted to make sure we were doing the right thing, so we took her to a psychiatrist when nothing else seemed to be working. Susie was also quite private about her struggle with depression and I didn't want to pry. Besides, I didn't know how to broach the subject.

Other than sending her to a psychiatrist, all I could think to do was spend time with her and do little things to cheer her up. During one pretty bad bout, I was searching for something that could lift her spirits. I knew she admired the Alfa Romeo, a very popular Italian sports car at the time, and made a mental note to look into pricing. I was partial to the Alfa Romeo because it's Italian. I figured Susie would appreciate that as well.

When my mechanic told me about a new Alfa Romeo possibly coming up for sale, I was overjoyed at the prospect of buying one for Susie. My children took after me in their appreciation for cars. Especially Susie. Lisa was less particular, but Susie preferred whatever was toughest and fastest. Sure, usually Susie liked driving around in a truck, but she also loved speed and sports cars. Maybe this gorgeous car is just the thing to help her get through a funk, I thought.

Eventually, we landed a hit – my mechanic told me the dealership next door would get a new one the next day. Without missing a beat, I made an appointment to go see it and drove over to pick up Susie the next day. Her whole face lit up with a huge smile when I told her the good news.

I'd already spoken to the mechanic and told him that I wanted to buy it. But right when we came in the next day, he took me aside and told me that this particular car actually had an issue with the motor, which he'd only just found out. This news seemed odd, because it was supposedly brand new, but I trusted the guy and decided I'd better not buy it. When I told Susie about this, I felt bad and apologized.

"That's okay, Dad. I'm used to disappointments," she replied ambivalently. I found that a sad and odd thing for someone her age to say. Then she changed the subject and invited me to come see the animals she was volunteering with through Farmers of America.

"Sure, let's go," I said. I was interested to see what her Animal Husbandry certificate program involved. It was a Sunday and no one was there, except Susie, taking care of the animals. There was a steer she took care of every day, who she named Duke. As I watched her, I thought to myself: Who does that? I didn't know anyone else who would take the time to volunteer with farm animals, but found it so endearing that she did. Lisa and she always loved their dogs growing up and were always attentive and loving to them.

Susie and I still went on our adventures on occasion. She was very social and didn't have as much time to spend with her dad, which I understood. Most twenty year olds aren't eager to go on outings with their parents. But we still had our fun and I felt like a kid again when we were having one of our father-daughter days. Susie was a sharp shooter and we often playfully competed to see who was the best shot. At the end of one of our shooting trips, she put the guns away and I checked the boxes, noticing one of the handguns was missing.

"Susie, where's the other gun?" I asked.

"Oh, I'm going to keep that one for my protection, since I live alone," she replied. I knew she handled a gun well and wanted her to feel safe, so I said that would be fine.

Susie and I also went on long drives and out boating, on occasion. I eventually bought her a boat because she enjoyed being out on the water so much. Sometimes, when I got off work early, I'd just call her up and ask if she wanted to join me for dinner. When Lisa was in town, I would call her and invite her as well.

After wrapping up modeling and college, Lisa went to graduate school and got engaged to her college sweetheart, Andy. For a brief period I had Susie, Lisa, and Andy working in my home office, processing paperwork and scheduling. Lisa and Andy married after graduate school and naturally, I wanted to throw them a nice wedding. We had the ceremony in Malibu at Pepperdine University's quaint, beautiful church, which sits on a hill with sweeping ocean views. The party afterwards was at Beaurivage, a fancy, popular restaurant that also boasted stunning ocean views. I always made sure a party I gave was a good time, and this was no exception.

Lisa modeling

I brought my serious girlfriend, Sheila, as my date. Sheila was an engineer who graduated from Stanford. Being of Persian decent, she was quite in touch with her culture and was an expert at certain traditional dances, which her mother had her show me. Things got serious quickly and we were talking about marriage, which was a huge deal for me. Once her extended family found out we were nearly engaged, they wanted me to come visit them in Iran.

A few weeks after Lisa's wedding, I stood at JFK, waiting to board the next flight to Tehran. I looked for any updates on the status of the flight while fighting off anxiety about the pending voyage – it would be the longest flight I'd ever been on, by far. A friendly voice came on the speaker and cheerfully announced that for some mechanical reason, they had to add a stop to my flight, which would be in Iraq. This is all getting to be too much for me, I thought. Another stop! I sat down at a nearby bar and considered my options over a drink. Within an hour, I bought a ticket back to LA. With a sense of dread, I realized I didn't have her family's phone number and had no way to let them know I wasn't coming. Sheila and her family waited at the airport for me and I didn't show.

A week or so later, Sheila showed up at my door in the Palisades. She wanted to talk. I was surprised to find that she was still interested in me, though she was upset about my cancellation. But it was already over at this point; the decision to turn around made me realize I didn't love her enough to marry her. The relationship slowly disintegrated in the way it typically did: I stopped calling. She quickly got the message.

CHAPTER 34

Haunting Me

———

ON ONE OF MY ROUTINE visits to my mom's, I was surprised to find Susie there as well. My mom was gushing over some photographs. Susie sat next to her, looking uncharacteristically embarrassed.

"What ya got there, Ma?" I asked her.

"Look, Joey!" she smiled at me and handed me some photos. I took the first one and saw it was a glamour shot of Susie. Surprised, I didn't know what to say. They were stunning, but threw me for a loop. Susie didn't do this sort of thing – getting dressed up and glamorous.

"Are you modeling?" I asked her.

"Started a while ago," she said. That was news to me. As far as I knew, only Lisa took an interest in modeling. I flipped through the photos, impressed that Susie could transform herself for a photo shoot. She was a tomboy who loved sports and driving around in her truck. And by this point, I suspected she was gay. Over the past couple of years, she'd had a few female friends who seemed to be more than a typical friend. She hadn't come out to me, though. In any event, I didn't care. Neither did Pat or Lisa. We just wanted her to be happy.

My mom kept trying to take all the photos for herself as Susie attempted to explain that she needed most of them. My mom acted like she didn't understand and I amusedly wondered whether or not she was using her broken English as an excuse to hoard all the photos.

Susie Modeling

"Ma, Susie has to keep most of those," I said eventually and Susie gave me a look of gratitude. "Let's eat dinner. I'm starving." We had a nice night, though I was a bit concerned about Susie. She was still seeing a psychiatrist and recently started taking Prozac, an antidepressant that had surged in popularity. I heard she had just gone through a breakup, but didn't know any details. Things seemed to be a bit better with her, though I could never quite tell because she didn't talk much about her mental health.

Less than a week later, I woke up from a deep sleep as my doorbell rang repeatedly. I blinked my eyes open, completely groggy. It was the middle of the night. As a doctor, I was used to getting calls at odd hours – but not visits to my house.

I fumbled for the light and got up, wondering who the hell was at my door. I swung it open and saw my son-in-law, Andy, standing there, his shoulders slumped, his face pale.

"Joe," he said softly. "I need to talk to you." His voice broke a bit as he spoke.

"What's going on?" I asked, alarmed. "Come inside." Andy came in and told me I should sit down. My entire body was in high alert, the worry welling up in my chest.

"What's wrong? Is Lisa alright?" Andy looked like he'd seen a ghost and hesitated to respond.

"Please, can we sit down?" he asked, his voice cracking. Exasperated, I sat down on the couch. Andy sat on the chair in front of me.

"It's not Lisa. It's Susie..." he trailed off, seemingly on the verge of tears.

My breath stopped and my heart felt like it was imploding. I instantly knew what he was going to say next.

"She's gone, Joe," he said solemnly.

The wind was knocked out of me and it took me a few seconds before I felt I could catch my breath.

"No," I uttered, barely able to speak.

"I'm so sorry," he said. "Everyone is at Pat's, waiting for the police." Without saying a thing, I ran to the counter, grabbed my keys, and ran out the door to my car. I sped over to Pat's house, my heart racing, in a state of sheer disbelief.

The second I saw her, I knew it was over; I knew she was dead. She was on the floor of the back house, lifeless. In that moment, my mind emptied and my chest felt like it would split in two. I slowly walked over to her and sat down, my eyes locked on her. I held her cold hand. I noticed a gun at her side – the gun she had taken a few months before. To protect herself.

I sat there in silence, feeling a pain unlike any other, a pain far worse than I knew was possible. It was as if my soul was slowly being ripped out of me. I have no sense of how much time went by, but eventually the police came and gently told me I had to leave the scene. I mechanically walked around to Pat's house and we sat together and cried.

Although our marriage ended shortly after it began, the hostility had greatly dissipated over time and we eventually came to somewhat respect each other, though there was still lingering anger. But in this moment, after seeing our lifeless daughter, none of the mistakes I had made in our marriage mattered. Truly, nothing else mattered. Our entire world had crashed down. There was nothing to say and nothing to do other than to try and keep existing.

I spent that night at Pat's house. In the middle of the night, I woke up and felt pulled to write something about Susie. I turned on the light, found a notepad, and sat down at the kitchen table to write a poem. It had to do with Susie driving her truck.

That was the worst night of my life. For a long time, most of that night seemed to be blocked from my memory; it was so dark and tragic that my mind seemed to want to protect me from its indelible, caustic pain. The days, weeks, and months that followed were grim. Susie was a ray of hope in my life. She had a certain light in her that I never saw in anyone else. Lisa has a distinct light in her as well, and I don't know what I'd do without her; I think I always knew losing either one of them would break me. I just never thought I'd lose a child. Whatever life threw at me, I could survive knowing my kids were alive and well. After losing Susie, I didn't have the same resilience to life's most challenging obstacles.

Maybe I saw my younger self in her, in a way – that little boy who was insecure and scared, but had a big heart. Helping her, in a way, was like helping myself too. I suppose that, in general, when we help another, we're also helping ourselves. But with her, it was even more so, because she was my baby and also mirrored the boy in me who struggled.

Like many people who lose a loved one to suicide, I felt a need to know *why* she killed herself. Some things were clear – Susie had a very challenging time with her dyslexia, of course. And though we hadn't openly discussed it, I knew she was gay. I didn't care who she dated, so long as she was kind to my daughter. If my kids were both happy, I felt happy. I desperately yearned for the laughter and joy that filled our house when she was young – before kids started making fun of her and before she was burdened with the weight of a learning disability and a homophobic society. The spectrum of emotions I felt after her loss was extreme, but grief and regret remained the strongest. I will always regret that I didn't spend more time trying to heal Susie myself.

As we spoke to Susie's friends, we learned there was more. Shortly before she died, her girlfriend broke up with her. Some of her friends also admitted that Susie had mentioned wanting to kill herself, but they hadn't thought she was serious. Now they were racked with guilt. They felt a need to tell us this in the hope that we might bring it up at the funeral, as a warning for others to take such comments at face value.

Pat's sister, Aunt Sue, handled most of the planning for the funeral. Susie had been like a daughter to her too – she had raised her for years, on and off, with Pat after the divorce. Susie was also named after her. I was a basket case in the days following her death, but fortunately Aunt Sue stepped up and did most of the planning and organizing. Pat also did a lot of the decision making. I don't even know who picked out the casket. I was so beside myself I could barely tell up from down.

Aunt Sue suggested we meet with her rabbi, Rabbi Rome (she had married a Jewish man and was learning more about the religion), who was also a psychologist. I took an instant liking to him and given that Pat and I weren't very religious, it was nice to have a man of a different faith who seemed open-minded about our wishes for the ceremony. It was important to us that we were transparent about the nature of Susie's death. We didn't want to keep that out of the ceremony or try to hide it in any way. We wanted to share openly with our friends and family, hoping to show them how catastrophic suicide is and how people should watch out for certain signs of it.

Shortly after Susie's suicide, I was shocked when one of her friends approached me and told me that she was worried another one of her friends, who had also been close to Susie, might commit suicide herself. As a doctor, I'm able to put a seventy-two hour hold on someone who is mentally ill, and I did so without hesitation. Her friend got help and was fine after some time. I was touched when she later gave me a sign that said, "Susie: Nobody loves you like your daddy loves you."

Another one of Susie's good friends seemed to blame himself in some way for the suicide; I suppose he felt guilty that he couldn't prevent it. I thought his sense of guilt was nonsense, but was seriously worried about him, so I told him I'd pay for him to see Rabbi Rome for therapy if he wanted and was glad when he took me up on the offer. I wanted to do anything I could to help Susie's friends and prevent them from going into a deep depression.

Before the funeral, we had a wake with a closed casket. A group of Susie's closest friends stood around it and I got a sense that many of them couldn't actually believe that she was gone; it was just so shocking. I stepped into the other room at one point, to have a few moments alone, but after a while, I heard a bit of commotion coming from the room with the casket.

"What the fuck are you doing?" I heard one girl ask.

"Don't touch that!" Another chimed in. Alarmed, I hurried back.

"What's going on?" I asked, concerned. The girls all stood there, surprised. I saw that the flowers that were draped over the top end of the casket had slid down toward Susie's feet. One of her friends, Katy, seemed like she'd been tampering with the casket. Confused, I looked up, waiting for an answer.

"Um, Katy was trying to look in the casket," one of them began timidly. "She can't believe Susie is gone...so she wanted to see with her own eyes..." she trailed off. There was complete silence.

"Does anyone else want to see her?" I asked, quietly. A number of girls nodded their heads. I thought about it for a few moments. "I'll open it briefly, for those who want to see her," I said. Though I worried about how they would react, I understood that some of them felt a need to see her body, in order to believe their friend was gone. And I didn't want to deny anyone that sense of closure.

I slowly opened the top part of the casket and once again saw what was left of my Baby Sue. She looked nothing like herself. She was lifeless, pale, had makeup on, and was in a frilly dress that she never would have worn. But by far the worst part was how her head was distorted from the gunshot. I stepped back and let her friends look, if they wanted to. I heard crying and some gasps as they approached the casket.

One of her best friends, Mare, walked up and seemed horrified by the sight. But she stood there and touched Sue's hands, which were crossed over her heart. Then Mare looked at her own wrist and fumbled to take off the bracelet she was wearing. She put it on Susie's wrist and tried to close the clasp, but seemed unable to, due to her trembling hands. Instead, she tucked it under each side of Susie's wrist. At the time, I didn't know that Mare had ever been romantically involved with Susie. But many years later, I found out that she and Susie were each other's first love. They fell in love when Susie was seventeen.

The funeral the next day was an outpouring of grief. I was oblivious to the audience, but Rabbi Rome later told me it had been standing room only at the church. Once she was buried, people couldn't keep away from her grave. I certainly couldn't.

Susie left a tape, which I've only watched a few times because it's so painful to see her talk about why she wanted to die. We let her friends watch it with us after the funeral. Susie also left a note that explained why she ended her life and her last wishes. She wanted her truck to go to one of her friends and her boat to go to her ex-girlfriend. We honored all of her wishes. She also absolved the psychiatrist she worked with, saying that it wasn't his fault. I didn't blame the psychiatrist. Susie had hidden how bad she felt. I had no idea it was anywhere near as dire as it was.

Lisa shared that, a few months before Susie's death, she had been looking for something in Susie's place when she saw a box with a journal in it. Her first instinct was to open the journal and take a look at it, but then she told herself she couldn't – it would be an invasion of her sister's privacy. Some time after Susie's death, she remembered the journal and read it, which was difficult to read both literally and emotionally. Because of Susie's dyslexia, her writing was often jumbled and difficult to decipher. But Lisa could make out enough to realize that Susie had been contemplating suicide for a long time. Lisa was startled to read her mention wanting to kill herself but being unable to because it was too close to Lisa's wedding date. We never knew how bad it was. Neither did her psychiatrist. Lisa wished she had only read that journal. "Maybe we could have stopped it," she lamented.

When someone commits suicide, everyone wonders what drove them to that depth of despair. I wanted to get to the bottom of it. Susie had been picked on since she was little, but she also had a group of kind friends who defended her. Everyone, other than the kids that bullied her, loved Susie. There was something about her that simply drew people in and comforted them, as if they instinctively knew Susie was warm, big-hearted, and innocent.

Shortly after the suicide, I sat my son-in-law, who is a psychologist, down.

"Why do you think she did it?" I asked. Andy looked at me with heavy eyes and waited a moment before speaking.

"The girl had too much against her, between the dyslexia and being gay... she just had too much against her."

In addition to the learning disability and her sexuality, Susie had a few failed relationships that really broke her down. As time went by and I considered the reasons for the suicide with many people, it seemed that the fear that she might end up alone was the straw that broke the camel's back. Of course, it wasn't any one thing that led to her final choice; there were many reasons she took that tragic path. It was incredibly difficult being gay in the eighties. Then there was the dyslexia and the medications she took. Even if the medication decreased the depression (which I'm not sure it did – some people think it made things worse), there was a huge stigma against antidepressants back then. It wasn't like today, where you see ads for an antidepressant every commercial break.

It's amazing how much society and the world have changed since Susie died in 1989. At least in liberal areas like Los Angeles, many (if not most) people are supportive of gay rights. In Susie's time, there was a huge stigma, which could lead to harassment, even violence. And gay people weren't featured in the media anywhere near as much as they have been in the past five to ten years. Young gay people barely had anyone to relate to or look up to. And very few of them felt they could come out, even to their own families.

The perception of dyslexia has changed entirely as the treatment and understanding of the disorder has dramatically improved. A few years after Susie died, the Olympian Bruce Jenner[3] opened up about his own struggle

---

3 The fact that Bruce recently opened up about being transgender and is now Caitlyn Jenner has also helped young LGBT teens accept their identities.

with dyslexia and became an inspiration to dyslexic kids. He certainly would have been an inspiration to Susie, given how much she loved sports and how great she was at anything athletic. But when Susie was alive, nobody was open about being dyslexic. People just didn't talk about it.

Later on, it became known that a slew of successful entrepreneurs were/ are dyslexic, such as Henry Ford and Richard Branson. Many dyslexic people are incredibly creative and gifted problem solvers, possibly because they are forced to figure out things with a significant impairment, which requires them to creatively find different ways to succeed.

Susie was talented in unusual ways. She was excellent with her hands and could fix practically anything. I'm still amazed that she could lay bricks like a professional after my dad showed her how to do it one time. The brick wall she built around my yard still stands today.

The memories continued flooding in, both the good and the bad. And in hindsight, I saw my mistakes like a flashing billboard: right in front of me and painfully obvious.

Memories of Susie taking care of her animals came up. I never saw anyone take care of animals with such tenderness and respect. When she was little, she wanted to be a vet. As she got older and school became more and more of a daily struggle, she stopped stating that dream.

Considering her academic struggles, I thought back to the time Susie was in high school and had a biology test the next day.

"This is really hard, Dad," she told me as she looked up from her textbook, appearing somewhat embarrassed. Susie hated to ask for help or to feel like she was a burden in any way. On that particular day, I had more time than usual and I could sense that Susie wanted me to help her.

"Let me take a look," I said, gesturing to her book. I flipped through her assigned pages and, of course, knew the material from back when I studied it myself in school as well as from the ongoing studies I did out of interest.

"I think I know what you'll be tested on!" I said excitedly, glad that I could help her out. I asked myself what I would ask on a test if I were the teacher, then started quizzing Susie on those items and explaining them in entertaining ways. As a teacher in the classroom, I always tried to tell students stories and make them laugh. There was no reason learning couldn't be fun, I figured. Besides, students seemed to learn best that way. Moreover, Susie and Lisa were my favorite people to bring laughter to.

A few days later Susie came running in excitedly and told me she got 90% on her test. I was so proud of her and gave her a hug. Then she said something that I glossed over, but that haunts me now.

"Why can't you do this for me all the time, Dad?" she asked, meaning why couldn't I help her study more often. I don't recall my reply, but I remember not realizing that she was essentially asking me, "Stay with me; teach me."

It breaks my heart now, to think of the time I could have spent helping Susie learn. I'm good at teaching and my daughters were the most important people in the world to me. For years I've berated myself about not spending more time helping to raise them. I still criticize myself about this. Back then, I thought I was spending a good deal of time with them, given my demanding work schedule and my busy social life.

Now I know that I could have done so much better. The hardest thing for me is feeling that maybe, if I had been a better father, I could have saved Susie. Of course, I will never know the answer to that. But the thought alone breaks my heart.

Grasping at ideas that could have saved her, I've even wondered if she would have stayed alive if I'd bought her that Alfa Romeo. Maybe it would have made her feel special enough to help lift her out of the depression, I thought. I've racked my brain about both large and small changes I could have made to help her.

There have been countless nights where I couldn't think of anything but Susie and the hole her absence left in my life. Nothing was the same once she was gone. I saw things differently. I became more introspective. I felt isolated because it was hard for me to talk about her loss; suicide is not something most people can relate to.

In some of my hours of despair, unable to sleep, I've walked into the center of my house and yelled out her name, in a cry of desperation. I'd call her name out several times, at the top of my lungs, as if somehow my relentless longing for her could bring her back, if only for a moment.

I would give anything to have her back. Although I endlessly dwell on my mistakes, I also often think back to Susie's childhood – how pure and playful she was. She was like an English sprite or a mischievous angel, running around in an Indian costume or dressed in her little league uniform with some black paint on her cheekbones, like a football player or a street kid.

I remembered a time when, out of the blue, Susie asked, "Dad, do you think you'll ever be famous?" She was a young teen at the time.

"Famous? What are you talking about, Susie?" I laughed, maybe reminded of myself as a kid and how I'd sit in the theater and imagine myself on the silver screen. But her question caught me off guard. When I reflected on that question after she was gone, I tried to remember what her reply had been, or if any more was said about it, but I couldn't recollect anything else. It hadn't seemed significant at the time. And maybe it wasn't, but when I recalled that comment after her death, it made me truly question what Susie most wanted out of life.

I wondered what could have made her truly fulfilled and happy. Though I'll never know for sure, I'm guessing the main thing may have been a partner she was really in love with, whom she could count on. I got the sense that she felt she couldn't completely count on anyone, even though I would have done anything for her, had I only known the state of things.

Many memories came back to haunt me. I thought back to the time Susie was a toddler yelling "I want my daddy" over and over again while I was at a conference. And how even as a little kid, she was a fighter. I think all her life she fought to stay alive and that all her life she had the fighting spirit, in spite of all the crap – the dyslexia and bigotry. As a child she didn't have to worry about those things. Every time I think of what she went through... I don't even want to think about it, because it just hurts me too much.

My mind also wandered back to the days where Susie, Lisa, and I would drive around in my Porsche, taking turns singing along on our microphone. I played those recordings and tears poured down my face as I heard my baby Sue singing along, without a care in the world, before anyone made fun of her and before she felt she didn't fit in. Before she felt rejected and worried she might not find a lasting partner.

One of the recordings was of me teaching her how to say, "Vroom, vroom," mimicking the sound of a motorcycle – a form of transportation that interested her since she was about two years old. "Brooooom, broom," she says on the recording. I heard myself repeating it back, making the rumbling sound of a motorcycle revving, then she'd do her best to imitate it.

The same recording blended into another scene: I was back east with Lisa and Susie at my mom's flat, after the failed attempt to get there by train. My cousin Johnny was there too. Just over the recording, you can get a sense of the cramped space and the warmth of everyone in it. My mom served us dinner and Lisa and Susie started play fighting, I assume, based on the sounds they were making. Then Susie cried briefly and I heard my younger self facetiously announce, "Everything is a crisis with these kids. Everything!" Johnny made some remark about how it was the same with his daughters. Susie's crying transitioned back into baby talk and I took the opportunity to try and teach her more phrases. And about halfway through the recording, I'm trying to teach her how to say, "I love you." I repeat it over and over again, as earnestly each time.

It struck me to hear myself saying "I love you" repeatedly, only because I was raised never actually hearing those words (although the sentiment was strongly felt, through my mom's actions). But I needed to say the words to her and Lisa countless times, almost as if I couldn't possibly express how much I loved them. The recording continued with me saying, "I love you. I love you. I love you," with a brief pause in between each statement, giving Susie a chance to repeat it. My mom, Johnny, and Lisa are talking in the background. And finally Susie says, "I love you" to the best of her ability and I'm taken back to that moment, one of the first times she told me she loved me, and am flooded with my love for her and the inconsolable grief from her loss.

CHAPTER 35

Finding A Way Forward

BREAKING THE NEWS TO MY mother was like reliving hearing it myself the first time. I waited a few days to tell her, to collect myself. When I told her, it was like I was watching what had happened to me – I saw a part of her die before my eyes. I hugged her as she wept uncontrollably. Stressed that she'd make herself sick, I started troubleshooting in my mind, thinking of what I would do if various things went wrong with her medically. In particular, I was truly afraid that she might go into a coma.

My mother was never the same after Susie died. Neither was I. In old times, we had been able to comfort each other. But it seemed nobody could really comfort anyone about this loss. I couldn't rely on my mom's support because she needed support herself. In a way, it was like everyone was on his or her own. I couldn't give Lisa the support she needed; I didn't even know how to. I certainly wanted to. Fortunately, Pat was better able to support Lisa. And Aunt Sue and Pat supported each other.

Over the years, Pat and I had grown a bit less resentful toward each other. But after Susie died, it was like any lingering resentment dissipated, at least for me. I can't speak to how she felt, although this change felt mutual. After something so tragic, the divorce was relegated to the past, a once incendiary memory that now could barely pierce the numbness we felt. In comparison to Susie's death, virtually no other past pain felt significant. So we put our differences aside and actually started to become friendly to one another.

I never stopped calling Pat my wife. Most people call a divorced spouse an "ex-wife" or "ex-husband." I never felt right calling Pat that, though. After all, neither of us ever remarried. It seemed cheap, in a way, to call her my ex-wife;

she was the only wife I ever had. So I still refer to her as my wife. There is a certain comfort to seeing Pat at family functions. We sit next to each other and there is a certain deep, unspoken understanding and respect we have for one another, despite all the heartache I caused. If nothing else, we both understood the loss of our child, which it seemed nobody else I knew could. Losing a child is the most painful thing a parent can experience.

I think it takes a tragedy to really appreciate what the soul is. Because once you lose someone, all you have left is her memory. And when that person is your child, it's like losing a part of your own soul. And that's all I know about it.

It felt like there was little more I could do than put one foot in front of the other at this time. I threw myself into my books. Although I was no longer working full-time, I had many friends and family members who consulted with me whenever they had a medical problem and besides, I enjoyed the reading. It seemed like the only healthy way to ease the grief was to immerse myself in science and art. Sometimes I was hanging by a thread and all I could do to stay afloat was read or close my eyes and listen to my favorite music.

Susie as a teen

A couple of years after Susie died, some good family friends of ours had their own tragedy that left their daughter in a vegetative state. Lisa, Pat, and I went to visit them one day. When we saw their daughter, Jenny, she looked like all the other vegetables I'd seen: almost lifeless, not at all herself, unconsciously hanging between life and death. But it occurred to me that at least she was *alive*. Her parents could still see her and spend time with her. As I sat there, looking at Jenny beside her parents, I turned to them and said, "At least you still have her." Lisa shot me a stunned look, silently gaping, but I wasn't sure why until we left.

"Dad, I can't believe you said that. That's God awful," she said. I hadn't even questioned what I said until Lisa mentioned it was inappropriate. I understood her point, but at the same time, felt maybe it was better to have their daughter alive, even in that state, than dead. At least they could see her and sit beside her.

CHAPTER 36

The Boards

AFTER SUSIE WAS GONE, I couldn't live the way I used to – carefree, going crazy on the social scene and dating an endless amount of women. Nor did I want to. I came to feel that, with my old behavior, I'd been doing an injustice to myself. It wouldn't take away from the pain I felt, anyway. I also realized that there were people, like some younger doctors I worked with, who looked up to me and I wanted to set a good example for them. After a while, I did date again and have relationships, but not with the same zeal. I spent a great deal of time alone, mostly studying science, eventually devoting myself to an old goal: passing the boards of internal medicine.

Despite working years as a medical doctor and saving many lives, I always had this feeling that until I passed the boards, I couldn't really consider myself a doctor. Now this isn't a standard I held anyone else up to and I knew that it wasn't necessary for a doctor to pass the boards in order to prove himself. In fact, I always stood by Father Luyet's belief that it wasn't the school you went to or your credentials that made you good at your job – only your actual performance could establish that. And I knew many wonderful doctors who never took the boards. Yet for whatever reason, I always wanted to pass the boards myself. Maybe because so many people thought I'd never even become a doctor, I felt I had to go above and beyond to prove what kind of doctor I could become.

In the past, I hadn't been able to take the boards, because I originally had a DO (as opposed to an MD) degree. But finally the opportunity opened up so I decided to take them. Though I studied hard, I didn't pass. Most of my colleagues (who were other DOs or MDs who used to be DOs) didn't attempt to take the test. "Why would you want to take that test? It's too hard," one colleague – and a doctor with a spectacular reputation – said to me. And he had a point. First of all, we had to take a test before we could take the boards – a test to see if we could qualify for *the* test, so to speak. And before the qualifying test, you had to be interviewed.

"Wow, they're really making us jump through hoops," I told a friend. I guess that's life – if you're not in the know, you jump through hoops. Despite the multi-level challenge, my friend Vic did pass on his first try. That was no surprise, as he was always far ahead of everybody.

I wasn't deterred by the initial test. I kept studying and in 1995, I finally sat down to take the boards again. Afterwards, I felt pretty good about it. When I found out I passed, I was elated. Looking at the sheet of paper that told me I was board certified, I finally felt like I was, irrefutably, a doctor. I drove over to see my mom, who knew that I had been studying hard for a test, but didn't understand the significance of it.

I looked at her and held out the letter, even though she couldn't read it, and said, "I passed the boards, Ma."

She clasped my hands in hers and said, "I'm proud of you, Joey."

My mom and I went back to Jersey to visit family and friends after I passed the boards. I was in a celebratory mood and hosted a bunch of people at my friends' restaurant, Goodfellas. My buddies had renamed their restaurant a few years back, after it was in Scorsese's film of the same name. The cheerleaders from high school came to the dinner and at one point, my mom started telling them about the young women I dated. "All these lollipops," she said with a sigh, rolling her eyes.

"Lollipops?" one of the cheerleaders asked. "Why do you call them that?"

My mom shrugged. "They're young and they're beautiful." Then she turned to me and in a firm voice, pointedly added, "Too young." Frustrated by the types of women I dated, my mom would occasionally suggest that I marry Dolores, the first girl I considered marrying.

"She's married, Ma. Has been for decades," I'd remind her. My mom was stubborn about many things and never gave up hope that I'd settle down with a woman she approved of.

The year after I passed the boards, I became an instructor at University of Southern California (USC), teaching med students how to do a proper medical history and physical exam. It was a delight to be in the classroom again; I always loved lecturing, especially about medicine. I grew close to my students and shared many real-world experiences with them from my years in the trenches. Mentoring the students was rewarding. Many of them asked me for overall career advice. The main thing I told them was to thoroughly study their physiology; to study not only because they had to, but to build confidence in their ability to help people. Otherwise, I'd say, get another profession because medicine is too important unless you completely commit. People need a doctor. They need someone to believe in.

As I taught, I always felt it was important to entertain the students and teach them through stories, as that is one of the best ways to learn something. If my stories could help make a medical lesson more memorable, then it could end up saving someone's life. There were also moments of levity. We joked around together. One group of students and I called ourselves the Seven Dwarves. I was Dopey.

Around this same time, a director friend, Richard Green, asked me to be in a movie of his, completely out of the blue. Surprised but honored, I said I'd be delighted to. It was called *Seven Year Zig Zag* and I played a rich guy dating a young, beautiful woman. My character eventually died of a heart attack. The movie never went anywhere, but it was fun to have that experience. I'd spent decades wondering what it would be like to act in a movie. A different friend of mine, Richmond Shepard, also asked me to be in a play of his. I had a ball playing the part of a corrupt lawyer in a performance of "Counselor At Law" in Santa Monica.

That same year, I found out I was going to be a grandpa. I was very excited to have a grandchild, but I was very upset by what they chose to name the baby. When we found out she was a girl, I made my request, which I assumed would be honored: I wanted her to be named Rose Marie, after my mother and my favorite aunt. In Italian culture, it's very typical for the father to choose the name and for the child to be named after a relative. When I found out the baby was going to be named Sophia, I was very displeased. But eventually I let it go because I was excited for my grandchild and I figured maybe the next baby could be Rose Marie or Joseph. I was denied again when I heard Lisa was going to name her second child Gabriel Harrison. This angered me more, because I wanted him to be named after my father and me. It's unheard of in Italian tradition, when the grandfather doesn't even get in the name. After finding out how disappointed I was, Lisa ended up naming him Gabriel Joseph Patrick ("Patrick" for Pat). I think Aunt Sue talked her into it.

Although I missed far too much of my kids' upbringing, Lisa seemed to get everything right as a mother. She's always been incredibly involved in their lives, from taking them to countless sporting events to helping them with homework, and everything in between.

Lisa, Sophia, and Gabe

CHAPTER 37

Priorities

I'VE ALWAYS DONE WHAT I can to help Lisa and my grandkids. Sometimes my friends are surprised by my generosity, but I don't understand their reactions. They're my family. What else should I be spending money on? Who would I be if I didn't pitch in to help out? A friend recently asked me if I would spoil my kids less if I could go back and do it over.

I paused and thought for just a second and said, "No, I'd probably spoil them more."

Everyone has different perspectives on what children should be given, but it's always been my role to help provide for everyone in my family. I started sending money to my mother once I got my first paycheck as an intern and continued to do so until she moved out to California. Once she moved, I provided her with housing, medical care, and anything else she needed until she died at 107 years old. It was the least I could do, after she raised me alone, working in sweatshops to pay the bills.

I visited my mother nearly every day in her final years. She remained stubbornly independent even as she turned 100 years old. Once word got around that my mom was a centenarian, people wanted to know the secrets to her longevity. Aging had long been one of my main areas of interest, so I started speaking about it. My lecture ended up being called, "Is there a fountain of youth?"

To help my mom out in those years, I let her stay in a condo in the Valley, although it would have been more convenient to have her stay in one of the several open rooms in my house in Malibu. But every time I asked her to live with me, she said it was too cold in Malibu. So we kept her place in the Valley.

As years went by, eventually she was nearly blind, but was still resolute in her decision not to have help. I would practically beg her to let me hire an aide for her, so I wouldn't worry about her falling all the time, but she refused. The next best thing I could do was set up a bunch of cameras so that I could periodically check that she was fine.

Around that time, she started saying "thank you" to me when I helped her out with things, even small tasks like getting her a cup of water. It struck me as odd at first; we had never said thank you; we simply showed our gratitude through our actions. It was also simply expected that we help each other; the appreciation was assumed. Yet for whatever reason, hearing her say, "Thank you, Joey" stopped me in my tracks every time. Boy, that broke my heart. She must have known she was dying.

My mom amazed people by living to 107. I'm very grateful my mom lived so long. People would often say it was incredible she lived to be that old, but I wished it could have been even longer. No amount of time is long enough when you dearly love someone.

Shortly after my mother's death, I got a call from Nancy. We hadn't spoken in many years – after some fight that neither of us could remember by this point – but she broke the ice to offer her condolences; she was genuinely worried about how I would be faring after the loss. I appreciated her gesture and immediately felt comfortable confiding in her about my grief. We quickly became friends and were able to laugh at old relationship memories that had once been so painful.

"Remember how you used to call me 'Nancy #1'?" she asked me one day over lunch.

"Yes! You're still Nancy #1," I replied, intending to compliment her.

"I thought you meant that I was the number one person in your life. It took me years to realize that I was Nancy #1 but that there was also a Nancy #3, 4, 5, 10, and 15," she said with a trace of sadness.

"Yeah, but you were number one!" And somehow, now we could laugh about it. As I started making amends with Nancy, I realized I wanted to make amends with other people I'd hurt in the past, like some of my other ex-girlfriends, but mostly Pat and Lisa.

I still talk to Pat and Lisa about how much I miss Susie. When I talk about her in this way, I often can't help but cry. It's a sorrow nothing and no one can ameliorate.

"I could have done better," I would often say to my wife. "So much better. I wasn't there enough." Usually this statement was met with silence, which I accepted. I knew it was true.

But one time Pat looked at me compassionately and replied, "We all could have done better." That caught me off guard. It hadn't occurred to me that she might have felt that way. I appreciated her sharing her opinion because it made me feel a bit more connected to the rest of the family, even if only through mutual regret. Pat seems to be better at grieving than me. She tells me that I'm missing a lot in the present when I spend so much time dwelling on the past.

"Joe, we will never forget Susie," she says. "We can't bring her back. As much as we all want to. We'd do anything to have her back, but it's impossible. But you do have another daughter. And two grandchildren. If you don't spend more time being present with them and appreciating them, won't that just be another regret?"

Pat is wise and I know she's right, but I don't know how to put the past pain aside. It controls me, in a way. When it surfaces, I often can't fight it off. It's like it lies right under the skin in my chest, ready to overtake me anytime, with no notice. Most of my friends are probably unaware of how much her loss still torments me. I know they realize her death is devastating, but I don't talk about it to them and I usually act like I'm doing fine, so they probably don't know how much it still stings. Reminders of her are everywhere, both intentional and otherwise. The walls in my room are covered with family pictures, mostly of her and Lisa. One of the pictures that she took right before she died always grips me. In her memory, I made a scholarship at the college she was planning to go to. And I did something else that I never told anyone about until recently. I picked a star in the sky and named it after her. I often look at that certificate and think of her star, wishing and praying that somehow, she knows how much I miss her and how much I love her.

CHAPTER 38

A Walk Up The Hill

IN 2004, AT SEVENTY-THREE YEARS old, I decided I wanted to formally work with patients again. After all, I still had my license as a doctor and although I didn't need or want to open another practice, I wanted to use my expertise to help people. Some of my doctor friends suggested I look into volunteering at the MEND (Meet Each Need with Dignity) Clinic, a medical center in Pacoima that serves underprivileged populations. I've been there twelve years now, going twice a month to spend the day working with people who can't afford healthcare.

A Hispanic woman in her thirties recently came in. Her name was Paula and she held out her hands, palms up, with her fingers half curled in what looked like a painful, stuck position. She started speaking in Spanish, clearly distraught. The clinic has a large population of Spanish speaking patients, so I always have an interpreter with me. That day's interpreter was Lily. As I waited for Lily to translate, I started going through all the possible causes for her ailment.

"She says there's been a problem with her hands," Lily started translating. "She can't really uncurl her fingers. She's been to doctor after doctor, place after place, and no one can help her. The doctors are barely giving her the time of day."

Looking into Paula's distressed eyes, I said, "Please, sit down. Let's see what the problem is." She seemed a bit relieved by my calm demeanor and sat down, her posture relaxing a little. I asked for charts from her previous visits, but she informed us that she had nothing. So I started from the beginning. I asked about the condition and began racking my brain trying to figure out what could be wrong.

After about thirty minutes of meeting with her, I still couldn't determine what was causing her fingers to curl. I told her that I would continue to study this issue and that I'd need to see her again next week. I thought she would be disappointed that I didn't have an answer for her. However, she looked at me with tender eyes and spoke to me in a tone that seemed to imply gratitude. I turned to Lily, curious to hear what Paula said.

"She wants you to know that every other doctor she's been to has rushed her and made her feel like another number. None of them gave her the time and patience you have. She asked why this place is different," Lily relayed.

My heart went out to Paula. This poor woman had felt like a piece of meat tossed around to different doctors who didn't have the time or desire to truly sit with her and listen. And I'm not blaming the doctors; that kind of treatment is a product of a flawed medical system – the majority of doctors no longer have sufficient time to spend with patients. I placed my hand on Paula's forearm and slowly said, "We're different because we love you." I noticed tears start to form in her eyes. Then I saw Lily was starting to cry as well. I felt a tear start to well up in my own eye, but I wouldn't show it.

After volunteering at MEND for a while, I decided I wanted to get involved in an additional medical organization. A colleague of mine told me about the Board of Governors at City of Hope, a non-profit research center and hospital that does some of the most advanced research to fight cancer. The first time I heard about City of Hope as a doctor, it sounded vaguely familiar and I tried to remember where I'd heard it before. Then it hit me – a buddy of mine and I had crashed a City of Hope gathering when I was in grad school. Ironically, I ended up joining City of Hope's Board of Governors about fifty years later. When they asked me to introduce myself, I got a lot of laughter when I told everyone about how my friend and I had wandered into a City of Hope event in our early twenties. "Finally," I said as I ended my introduction, "I can stand up now and truthfully say I'm a new member."

I still read about science and medicine every day. When I'm reading these subjects, I go into a state where the rest of the world is shut out. It's just me and the book and the knowledge. Time and daily stresses generally fade away as I analyze what I'm reading and question what its implications will be in the future. That's still how I spend most of my time: studying medicine. I continue to volunteer at the clinic, so it's imperative that I keep up with new discoveries. But even if I weren't practicing, I'd still be studying – simply for the sake of knowledge, because science has fascinated me for well over seventy years.

Often times, during my reading, I'm interrupted by the phone. If it's a good friend, I'm pleased. If it's a telemarketer, I'm pissed. I talk on the phone with Lou and Sharon the most often. When I talk to them, it's as if no time has passed; we slip right back to where we were the last time we saw each other. And sometimes I'm pleasantly surprised to get a call from a former student or someone I mentored. A former student, Cecilia, recently called to check in.

"What are you up to, Joe?" her familiar voice asked.

"I've been reading a new book on genetics," I started. "How are you?"

"I'm well. Tell me more about your book." Cecilia is like me – always interested in learning the latest about medicine. And anytime someone asks me about medicine, I'm uplifted to share some of my knowledge. It's like being back in the classroom teaching again, in a way.

I told her I'm doing different research on genetics, because that's where the future of medicine is.

"Why genetics?"

I explained that it's the therapy of knowing your genome so that you can properly take medications your doctor prescribes because, at this time, doctors can't know precisely what dosage is correct for each individual. "What's right for you and what's right for me would be different; it's different for everyone. The pharmaceutical companies put out an average dose, but the average isn't accurate for us as individuals."

"That's concerning."

"Tell me about it! It's been more than a decade since the first human genome was sequenced. It has become clear that no one – absolutely no one – is average." I continued on without pausing, because I knew she was interested and once I start talking about a medical topic of interest, it can be hard to stop. I tend to go into lecture mode. "Not everyone's genetic variances are likely to be profoundly impacted. But we shouldn't ignore those differences because we have tools where we can intervene in very personalized ways. Not every doctor has the tools and training to assist their patients like this. Many doctors don't even know they exist. But they should, because it's possible to kill a person just giving them a normal dose. It's rare – but it happens."

"How dreadful. It's a shame more doctors don't know that."

"That's why I read all these books; I'm up till one or two in the morning, then I get tired and sleep."

"What else do you see as important to the future of medicine?" she inquired.

"Well, I also see immunology as the future of medicine." I explained that immunology is the ability of the cells in the body to fight off infections and cancer, etc. Then I started reflecting aloud about the incredible medical breakthroughs we'll have. "We will master the science of immunology with all its intricacies and secrets and use stem cells to replenish the body's worn out tissues. I see great discoveries in terms of surgery, microsurgery, and transplantation. The future is very bright." Just then, I glanced at the muted television and saw the headlines about terror threats. "Provided we don't blow ourselves up," I added as a caveat. Like so many people, I worry about where our world is going, but I try to remain hopeful that humanity will have a positive trajectory.

After losing so many people I was close to, particularly Susie, I questioned life itself more than I ever had before. We all want to know what our lives mean. We live this life; we don't know why we're on Earth. We don't know if there is a supreme personal god. We don't know who's behind the universe. And if no one is behind it, how the hell did it happen? We probably never will know. When I ask myself what I can count on, I think back to certain moments of clarity. I think of the way I felt when I held my daughters for the first time. I think of the elderly couples I saw in my office who cared for their disabled mates. I think of how hard my mom worked to provide for me. And then I know there is one thing I can count on: love. The only thing we got in life is love. Love is the only thing life can't cheat us out of.

"I'd like to make a toast to Pat," I announced at my grandson's latest birthday dinner. "We're all here because of Pat. She was the one who decided to get pregnant and knew it would be a good idea to have kids. Wasn't even on my radar. I didn't even know I wanted children. But when Lisa was born, all of that changed. I had never felt such love for anyone as I felt for her when I held her for the first time." We made a toast, then I continued on, telling Gabe and Sophia why I was proud of them.

I'm glad that Pat and I are able to spend time together with the whole family, despite the divorce. Sometimes she even surprises me by saying something particularly kind. After Lisa and Andy divorced, Pat told me, "You know, you're 100 times better than Andy ever will be." I nearly fell out of my chair. Hearing Pat compliment me like that was a complete shock. "At least you still provide for the grandkids," she added.

Every now and then I still have to run my old camper, the one I have full of supplies. Usually I'll take it down to Lisa's to visit the family. The last time I drove over was for Easter. Pat was there too and we all spent the afternoon together. It's always a nice change to have the family all together. Sometimes it pains me to think about how those gatherings might occur much more frequently if my marriage had worked out.

Toward the end of the afternoon, Lisa and Pat were talking about something that the rest of us weren't terribly interested in. I suggested Gabe and Sophia join me for a walk. Gabe is about to graduate high school and Sophia is a sophomore in college, but I still call them "the kids" endearingly. We took our Sunday stroll and walked through the same streets where I used to go on weekend bike rides with Lisa and Susie. I felt a wave of sadness as I thought about how Gabe and Sophia never got to meet their aunt, but I didn't want to bring up something so heavy. So we spoke about everyday things: school, sports, and my work at the clinic. As we proceeded down the charming tree-lined streets in the Palisades, I felt the sadness lifting. There's something about seeing my grandkids that always brightens my day.

We took a path away from our street and walked up toward Sunset, the thoroughfare, and ended up walking up a little hill. I felt a bit winded on the way up and shook my head with a laugh as I watched my grandkids easily spring ahead of me. Once I caught up with them, we stood a few moments at the top and enjoyed the view of the nearby houses along the hills. It was an early spring and the usually brown hills were refreshingly green, with flowers blooming. I took in the fresh coastal air.

On our way back, I had them stop at the camper. "I want to give you something," I said, motioning for them to join me while I went into the camper and rummaged through my things to find a couple of gifts. The kids looked through all my supplies in curiosity. As Pat puts it, I have enough in there to survive any disaster.

Finally I found what I was looking for: some rolls of quarters and a special type of flashlight.

"Now, Gabe, Sophia," I began, "here's a roll of quarters. I know what you're thinking: 'What do I need quarters for?' but the truth is, you never know when you'll need change, particularly quarters. So keep these in your car," I said as I handed them each a roll of coins.

"Thank you," they said in unison.

"And here is a special flashlight – be *very* careful with it. It's strong enough to temporarily blind somebody, so never shine it in someone's eyes unless you need to defend yourself." Sophia and Gabe exchanged a knowing look and smiled back.

"Ok, Grandpa," Sophia said. "Thanks."

"Thanks, Grandpa," Gabe added.

The kids went inside ahead of me and showed Lisa and Pat what I'd given them. I also brought some quarter rolls in for my wife and daughter and handed one to each of them. After thanking me, Lisa asked the kids what else they had.

"Grandpa also gave us some new flashlights," Sophia said. I saw Pat smiling as if she were suppressing laughter.

"Another flashlight, just what you need," Lisa said playfully. Pat laughed but also smiled pleasantly.

"You never know when you might need an extra light. The power goes out occasionally. And this flashlight can be used as protection too – it can temporarily blind someone," I added.

"Be careful with those," Lisa said to the kids.

Although my ongoing gifts of survival tools have become a bit of a running joke in the family, I think Sophia and Gabe realize what I'm trying to do. I think I'm instilling in them a sense that you never know what's going to happen in life, so we should all try to be at least minimally prepared (and even then we'll inevitably be missing things). But I had to live my life, my whole life, that way. I had to rely on myself.

"Well, I should get going," I said. I was getting tired and figured it was time to head back home. I hugged each of them then started slowly walking out. I heard them chatting and thought about how fortunate my grandkids are to have such a loving mom and how Pat and I are so lucky to have Lisa and our grandkids. I briefly looked behind me to see them all smiling at each other and the warmth they had for each other was palpable. They smiled and waved at me and I waved back.

As I got in the car, I looked up at the little house where I'd had my happiest memories with Lisa, Susie, and my mother and felt glad I kept it, because it allowed Lisa to raise Gabe and Sophia in the same neighborhood. My life took a lot of strange turns. Most people, including myself, never would have thought I'd end up a successful doctor gallivanting around Hollywood. I made a lot of mistakes along the way, but I got some things right. And in other ways, was simply fortunate. A lot of my success was the product of hard work and some of it can be chalked up to the phenomenon of chance. I sure lucked out with my grandkids.

My grandma, Dona Grazia

Riding a pony as a kid

Celebrating New Year's Eve at Barcelona's Bar and Grill with Joe Bosco, Augie Sodora, Jig (the waiter), Micki Nisuta, and Sal "Jerk" Gardino

Before the Senior Social dance at Garfield High School, 1949

Posing by a car I liked with my college buddy, Fred Scielzo

Track Team 1952-5.. Coach Kenneth Mackenzie, right, second row, end.

The college track team, 1952. I'm in the front, second from right.

1/2/55

Dr. Sun, Cassy, Charlie

Some professors and a fellow student at St. Louis University

My father working in Port of Spain, Trinidad, 1966

My dad, me, and my mom on one of his occasional visits

Pat and me after our engagement

Susie in a costume

My cubs, Lisa and Susie

Me and Lisa

Sharon and Me at a Christmas party, 1973

Lisa and Susie getting ready for a riding lesson, and my mom

My mom and my granddaughter, Sophia

Me and my grandson, Gabe

Volunteering at the MEND Clinic

ACKNOWLEDGEMENTS

———

SO MANY PEOPLE HAVE BEEN my North Star and I wish to acknowledge them here.

Lou Russo and Horace DeTecco—my lifelong friends who collected cash around the neighborhood when I needed more money in order to continue medical school. Lou inspired me to take on the task of becoming a student. Horace was always there for me and always lent me a car.

Dr. Joseph Catania, who was the ideal family doctor, and the man who inspired my career.

Dr. Peter J. Debell, who was an eminent surgeon. I was privileged to be his scrub nurse, which allowed me to assist him during countless surgeries. All that experience gave me an edge when I went into medical school and certainly helped me throughout my years as a doctor.

I thank Father B.J. Luyet, Ph.D., and Sister Mary Pierre, Ph.D., for being like a father and mother to me at Saint Louis University. They taught me a great deal about biology, but more importantly, they taught me how to be a better man. Their devotion to science was admirable and inspiring.

The talented internist, Dr. Bill Eninstein. I went into internal medicine because of his leadership.

Dr. Rome, a psychologist and rabbi who was a good spiritual guide for me, even though I'm Catholic. He motivated me to strive to become a mensch.

Dr. Theodore Rich, a psychiatrist I saw who gave me better insight into myself.

Lauren Adamson, who came into my life and helped me share my story. I thank her for allowing me to be frank and honest without hesitation. I was lucky to work with someone talented, trustworthy, and empathetic.

Jacqueline Steltz-Lenarsky, who edited the manuscript and gave valuable feedback.

I thank the following people for sharing stories with Lauren and me during the writing process: Sharon Richardson, my cousin Annabelle Zoda, Marlin Schwartz, Mike Appleton, Fred Scielzo, Lou Russo, Nancy Steele, Art Lucera, Mare, Susan Mizarhi, Gabriel and Sophia Stewart, and Pat and Lisa Turcillo. You have all touched my life and your memories helped shape this book.

And I thank the following people for reading a draft of the book and providing invaluable feedback: Sharon Richardson, Terry Adamson, Emily Laetz, Marie Gribble, Kate Paige Skeith Pincus, and Phil Riola.

I owe the most thanks to my family. To Pat Turcillo, who blessed me with two beautiful children, Lisa and Susie. I'm thankful to you for them and I'm also sure God is thankful to you. To my daughter, Lisa, who blessed me with two beautiful grandchildren, Gabriel and Sophia. And always, to my daughter Susie, who brought me joy whenever I saw her.

I'm also grateful for my wise sister-in-law, Susan Mizarhi, who can do a damn good impression of an Italian gangster. She's always been caring to the family and me.

And my father, who often said, "Hey, there's a lot of good in me, you know." I always appreciated his wit.

My grandmother, who made the best Sicilian pastries in the world and supported her family by working day and night.

My cousins Annie and Johnny, all my cousins in Toronto, and all my aunts and uncles on my father's side, who gave me a sense of family.

And to my mom, who was all I had for so many years. She went to work sick and all, so that I would be fed and clothed.

JOSEPH TURCILLO JR., M.D., F.A.C.P. was born in Hackensack, New Jersey. He received his BS from Fairleigh Dickinson University and studied biophysics at Saint Louis University. He received his medical degree from Kirksville College of Osteopathic Medicine in 1959 and moved to Los Angeles, California. There, he began a distinguished career as a physician and teacher of medicine. His numerous achievements and honors include being named Chief of Staff at Burbank Community Hospital  and cofounding its cardiopulmonary lab. These days, he volunteers to treat underprivileged patients and serves on the Executive Committee of the Board of Governors of City of Hope. He lives in Malibu, California and is a lifelong fan of Frank Sinatra.

Lauren Adamson, a writer, ghostwriter, and editor, received her BA in English from Santa Clara University and her MBA from Pepperdine University. She lives in Los Angeles.

62720114R00130

Made in the USA
Lexington, KY
15 April 2017